BEYOND LUCK

Practical Steps to Navigate the
Path from Manager to Leader

JOHN E. LANGHORNE, PH.D.

Beyond Luck

Created and printed in the United States of America.

Published by the Corridor Media Group
845 Quarry Rd.
Coralville, IA 52241

ISBN 978-0-615-33791-3

Library of Congress Cataloging-in-Publication Data
Control Number: 2009942933

The author and publisher assume no responsibility for errors, inaccuracies, omissions or any inconsistency herein.

First printing 2010

Editor: John Kenyon, Corridor Media Group
Cover design and layout: Jill Colbert, Corridor Media Group

For ordering information or special discounts for bulk purchases, please contact the Corridor Media Group at 845 Quarry Rd., Coralville, IA 52241 or (319) 887-2251. E-mail: info@corridorbiznews.com. Web: www.corridorbiznews.com

For more information about the book or the author, contact John Langhorne Associates, 1508 Buresh Ave., Iowa City, IA 52240 or (319) 354-2686. E-mail: jlanghorne@mchsi.com. Web: www.langhorneassociates.com or www.beyondluck.net.

To leaders and managers everywhere.
Your efforts guide the organizations that deliver the
services and products that better our lives – thank you.

For Mary Jo and Jyl for suggesting this book over and over.

To: John Lohman, who started the Corridor Media Group and made
this possible, first by creating the *Corridor Business Journal*, inviting
me to contribute to the Tree Full of Owls column and suggesting that
this material would be of value to leaders and managers everywhere.
John Kenyon, who performed the yeoman's task of thoughtfully and
sensitively editing every facet of this book. Jill Colbert, who brought
her design and organization excellence to craft the copy you hold.
Lynn Manternach of Mindfire Communications Inc., who gently
pushed me toward an understanding of branding and social media.
The leadership-development groups that have participated with me in
multi-year forums of reading, discussion and reflection on leadership
and management. The Iowa City Area Chamber of Commerce,
where I have had the opportunity to hone my understanding of leadership during 20 years of the Community Leadership Program. The
reviewers who gave of their talent and time to help refine this un-
book. And most importantly, to the many clients I have worked with
who have shaped my philosophy and practice by showing me the
good, the bad, the ugly and the exemplary.

Thank you all.

John C

BEYOND LUCK:
Practical Steps to Navigate the Path from Manager to Leader

Introduction: How not to Read this Un-Book

Overview of Management and Leadership

UNIT 1: MANAGEMENT PRACTICES

UNIT 2: MANAGEMENT PRINCIPLES

UNIT 3: LEADERSHIP AND EXECUTIVE BEHAVIOR

UNIT 4: MOTIVATION AND MORALE, JOBS AND JOB LOSS

UNIT 5: PERSONAL DEVELOPMENT

How not to Read this Un-Book

This book is designed to provide you with short, explicit ideas and tools to help you become a better manager, executive or business owner/executive. It is also designed to allow you to read as briefly as you may need to or to delve deeply into a particular area of interest.

In its makeup, however, this is not a traditional book. It is more like a printed version of a web site, a collection of relatively short segments grouped by content and cross-referenced to help you explore additional relevant material. Most of the articles are about 800 words long and most of us read about 250 to 500 words per minute with 50 percent comprehension (so if you really want to nail the information, you need to read it at least twice or more). Many of the articles offer practical "how to do it" advice. I doubt that anyone will ever read this book from cover to cover.

It has five units of material on:
1. Management Practices
2. Management Principles
3. Leadership and Executive Behavior
4. Motivation and Morale, Jobs and Job Loss
5. Personal Development

Each article has a **pullout** that summarizes the basic purpose of the article to help you assess its usefulness to you. At the end of each article is a **Go To list** that takes you to related material. So, start with any topic, like "Troubled and Troublesome Employees" (1.13), read it and follow the "go to" for more related material.

Who should use this book:
Manager with a particular people problem or in need of some ideas to become more effective: You can quickly identify explicit tools to use in most situations and then read further to understand the basic principles underlying these tools.

New manager or a manager interested in further developing skills: You can use these articles to develop a clear picture of what management is as well as learn some practical tools to become more effective as a manager.

Entrepreneur/owner: There are many ideas and tools that can help you get through the initial startup and help you to manage the challenge of scaling your business.

CEO or CEO/owner of a small or mid-size business or organization (< 5000 employees): You will find material that is appropriate to your role.

People-development manager: You can use this book to design, by choosing the articles and their sequence, a relatively good management-development program. It also contains some ideas about how to build the training program so that it is more effective than the usual talking at people type of training.

Person (manager or no) interested in improving your day-to-day performance in the workplace: There is material within that shows you how people succeed and fail and tools for doing the former. Begin by reviewing the titles of the Development Index.

In short, anyone in a managerial role in almost any type of organization will find practical ideas and tools that will help to improve performance.

How to start

I suggest you **begin with An Overview to Management and Leadership** to understand my philosophy and to understand the process of becoming a better manager or leader.

Then start with the five units and go to what interests you. If you have an "itch to scratch" and find a title, check the **pullout** and follow your itch. Every article has about three **go to** leads to supporting material.

Go to the **Topics Index** if there is some concept or practice of interest, such as group management, employee engagement or setting up a quality process, and choose an article to start. Browse the Topics Index and you may find some ideas here that you had not thought of as management.

If you are interested in practical ideas to improve your functioning or to coach others in the workplace, go to the **Development Index**.

If you have a particular people problem, go to the **Problem-Solving Index** and find the issue you are interested in there. Begin with the articles cited and then use the **go to** citations at the end of each article to read deeper or more widely about this or related issues.

Should you wish to go deeper into the subject, the **HBR Index** is an annotated bibliography of what I consider the best articles on management, leadership and organizations from the *Harvard Business Review*. These articles are much longer and are available online at http://hbr.harvardbusiness.org for a nominal cost. The list has been tested with small groups of executives in a multi-year leadership-development process that uses this list as the basic reading material.

Management

"The fundamental task of management is to make people capable of joint performance by giving them common goals, common values, the right structure and the ongoing training and development they need to perform and to respond to change."
- Peter Drucker

Perhaps the simplest definition of management is **getting people to do things for you**. Another short and explicit definition is **getting work done through people**. Both of these definitions make it clear that management is about people and that to become an effective manager you must reflect on this fact, believe it and practice it.

My favorite is that **management is a principle-driven art**. This definition makes explicit that management is driven by principles and that excellent management is principled. There is evidence that principle-driven behavior is more flexible, consistent and effective than many of the "by guess and by gosh" practices that I encounter as a consultant. It is also important to appreciate that effective management practices are guided by a healthy dose of common sense and that sometimes common sense is in short supply.

Excellent management is hard work. There is not a "silver bullet" that will solve all of your problems. You must have a repertory of skills supported by an understanding of basic principles.

Obviously, management requires that managers have tools and techniques to use in their day-to-day work lives. Let me caution that every tool and technique in this book can be and has been used by thoughtless managers to create havoc and uncertainty, abuse people in the workplace and aggrandize the power of the manager.

Management is a learned skill. The principles of management are explicit whereas the practice of management is experiential. Management is learned through action, assessing the results of the action, reflecting on how to improve and acting again. Becoming a manager is an iterative process of trial and error guided by principles and techniques.

I am often asked if anyone can become an effective manager. The answer is no. Many people do not have the values, beliefs, interpersonal skills, courage and persistence to become effective managers. For an excellent overview of the transition into a manager role, see *Becoming the Boss* in the HBR Index.

Leadership

"Managers do things right, leaders do the right thing."
- Peter Drucker

If you Google the above quote, you will get more than 500 hits. If you repeat this process with leadership, you will get more than 1.5 million hits — have a good read.

If management is a principle-driven art, leadership is much more ambiguous. The literature on leadership strongly indicates that the most compelling characteristic of leadership is the absence of any shared characteristics. Leaders appear to have a deep intuitive understanding of who they are and use this knowledge to maximize their performance. Interestingly, most leaders have a single or series of life crises, often referred to as crucibles, that have acted as a catalyst to initiate and energize this personal transformation.

There is a great deal of material in this un-book about leadership. Start with the first five articles in Unit 3 for an overview of some of the more important thinking on leadership, while 3.5 reviews what is known about the development of this essential character that is difficult to define but easy to recognize. Then, consider the eight articles (3.6-13) on Drucker's effective executive characteristics. After that, go to Unit 2 on principles, and pay particular attention to 2.1, 2.8 and 2.9. It is impossible to review leadership without an in-depth consideration of integrity and ethics (see 2.10, 2.11 and 2.12). Conclude this readings series with the five articles on executive wisdom (3.14-18).

Unit 1:
Management Practices

To become an effective manager, it is necessary to understand the basic principles that shape management practice. However, this alone is not sufficient. It is also necessary to have in your manager repertory a set of concrete practices that you can apply in your role as manager. These practices, together with the principles, give you the basis to develop and refine your management skill.

Much of management is a combination of thoughtful planning and timely execution. Execution provides immediate feedback on the results of your actions and analyzing, and reflecting on this information is a tool to improve your management skills. You cannot become an outstanding manager by studying this book, but you can become an outstanding manager by applying the practices and principles in this book, considering the results of these practices and continuing to refine your skills.

The intent of the first two chapters is to juxtapose practices and principles. I have placed practices first because generally managers want to get to the "what to do" part as quickly as possible. You can go the topics in Unit 1 to find advice, sometimes very explicit, on "How to..." and then consult the underlying principles in Unit 2 that provide the foundation to support your practice.

Unit 1 is generally organized as a progression of practices, from very basic and necessary skills, such as how to give feedback, to more complex skills, such as how to carry out an effective performance review. Start with a topic you are interested in and then use the "Go To" at the end of each segment to guide you to related or supporting topics.

This chapter has three parts:

Nine segments that give explicit advice on how to do the most fundamental management skills. They are organized in a logical, developmental sequence.
1. The Basics of an Effective Management Style
2. One-on-One Feedback Is Vital for Your Employees
3. Improving Your Communications through Active Listening
4. KISSing and Chunking: A Magical Method for Better Communications
5. Candor Is a Valuable Trait in Successful Leaders

6. Coaching to Improve Performance
7. To Improve Productivity, Try Saying Thank You
8. Managing Better Meetings
9. Beware: Change Imposed Is Change Opposed

Four segments that introduce more advanced practices that require the basic skills of the first section and are focused on one-on-one practices.

10. Making Performance Appraisal Work
11. Bottom-up and 360° Feedback
12. Employee Attitude Change: Fishing and Zapping
13. Managing Troubled and Troublesome Employees

Four segments that introduce more sophisticated practices. If you are interested in making change, pay particular attention to the internal customer segment.

14. Using Skip-Level Meetings to Sense the Organization
15. Optimizing Your In-House Training Programs
16. Why Most Employee-Recognition Programs Don't Work
17. Driving Quality Improvements with the Internal Customer Model

The Basics of an Effective Management Style

It is clear from research and experience that some management practices are winners whereas other are losers. Many of us have had the opportunity to work for the "manager from hell," and such a person's dysfunctional characteristics are well understood. Examining these is a valuable exercise in reviewing and further enhancing our own management styles.

There are three core characteristics that contribute significantly to the poor performance of any person in the workplace, and this is particularly so for managers who use these practices. Poor managers tend to be:

Secretive. Secrecy is a canker that eats the soul out of organizations. It breeds distrust, fear and paranoia. Secrecy as a management practice gives rise to the view among employees that the organization practices "mushroom management" — I must be a mushroom, because people keep me in the dark and feed me BS.

We know the grapevine is a sensitive measure of the emotional tone of the organization and that effective managers are always sensing the state of the grapevine. A secretive organization has a very negative grapevine. Such a grapevine will be filled with vicious gossip, innuendo and unkind speculation about people and the company.

Punitive. I once worked with a person whose basic philosophy of dealing with people seemed to be "never let a cheap shot pass." Such a person is very difficult to work with and has a powerfully negative effect on our self-confidence.

A secretary interviewed during an organizational assessment would awaken feeling ill every Monday morning and occasionally she would even throw up. I had no idea what was causing this problem until I met her boss. He was one of those ultra-critical persons who communicated to people that every piece of work they did was inadequate. Such a person just grinds people down until there is nothing left of them. If you work for such a person, not only does your self-esteem decline but you also begin to question the worth of everything you do.

Unpredictable. It is possible to develop strategies to cope with secretive or punitive management styles. However, the most destructive management style in the workplace is unpredictability. Regardless of the personal and professional strategies we develop to cope with inconsistency, it is impossible to learn the rules of behavior because they are always changing.

In interviews with employees, they often report that the hardest type of manager to work for is one where each morning you have to assess "What mood is s/he in today?" Human beings are creatures of habit and as such we need consistency in both our personal and professional lives. Unpredictable behaviors render people helpless because they cannot develop ways to gain control over their environments.

Unfortunately, many of us have had the dubious opportunity to work for the 'manager from hell.'

In developing an effective management style, it is important to formulate a basic principle for communication. One that I encourage managers to consider is: "The better informed people are, the better they function." Practicing such an open communications style sends a powerful positive message to your people about your level of respect for them and indirectly invites their input into issues and decisions.

It is difficult to build people up by tearing them down with criticism. Is there such a thing as constructive criticism? Many employees think not. Learning how to coach, counsel, train and mentor people is an essential skill for effective, respected managers. Yet most employees note that the only time they hear from the boss is when it's bad news. For starters, consider the coaching strategy from the best-selling management book titled *Zapp: the Lightning of Empowerment*. Use this coaching tool and you will rapidly develop a reputation as an effective manager.

Monitoring our own behavior is the key to maintaining consistency or predictability in the workplace. One of the most effective tools for doing this is the say/do ratio: I will do what I say I will do when I say I will do it. Do not over-promise and under-deliver. People are very sensitive to the say/do ratio and do not respect or trust people with low ratios. To keep yours as high as possible it is important to track your behavior. You can do this with telephone logs, appointment calendars, notebooks of things to do, to-do lists, Post-it notes, PDAs and other tools for self-communication.

Over years of working in organizations, I have compiled a list of managerial practices that employees find disrespectful and incompetent. Consider using this list as a private self-test. Answering yes to any one of these suggests you need to do some thoughtful reflection regarding your management style.

- Sarcasm (Latin root – "tearing flesh")
- Not listening, ignoring
- Sniping (talking about someone when you should be talking to them)
- Punishing or writing policies for "all" for one person's misbehavior
- Breaking confidence
- Asking for input when the decision has been made or on trivial decisions
- Not explaining why
- Writing a policy to solve a problem
- Coming to meetings late
- Multi-tasking or side-talking during a meeting
- E-mail offenses too many to enumerate

Research shows that the immediate supervisor has the greatest impact on employee attitudes and performance. Consistently showing respect for your people is a sure winner for managers. Always remember as manager it is far more important that your people respect you than like you.

Go To:
One-on-One Feedback is Vital for Your Employees (1.2)
Respectful Behavior (2.4)
Improving Your Professional and Personal Productivity (5.1)

One-on-One Feedback is Vital for Your Employees

In the past decade, the Gallup organization has begun to carry out extensive surveys of the American workplace. Their "Q12" survey is probably the best-designed and most statistically sound assessment of employee satisfaction in use. These 12 questions can give a comprehensive picture of employee attitudes across a wide range of work environments. In fact, *Fortune* magazine uses this survey to build its "100 Best Places to Work" annual issue.

A consistent and compelling finding of the Gallup surveys is that around 70 percent of employees say they rarely get feedback from their immediate supervisors. I am impressed that this finding has remained essentially unchanged since I began consulting two decades ago. This, in spite of countless seminars that preach that feedback improves performance. Ken Blanchard became a nationally known management guru by writing a book, *The One-Minute Manager*, that can be reduced to a sentence: Give your employees timely, accurate feedback about their performance and make sure most of it is positive.

An effective feedback process has five major elements:

Choose the time and place with care. Most employees prefer private one-on-one interactions, be they positive or negative. Never give negative feedback in front of peers or in public; this is a major morale killer. Always set people at ease by telling them the purpose of the conversation.

Describe as succinctly as you can the behavior, situation or event; make it clear to people what you are talking about. Vagueness is a trust killer. Make sure you are prepared and be economical and focused in your comments. Blah, blah, blah usually leads to confusion and miscommunication. Just because you are the boss does not mean that you can talk at people on and on; this will probably be seen as disrespectful.

When giving feedback to improve performance, perhaps the major omission by managers is a failure to concretely connect the event in question to its results. People need to understand that what they do or don't do has effects in the workplace and a characteristic of poor performers is

'I can live for two weeks on a good compliment.'

- MARK TWAIN

"I don't get this."

Probably the most important element is the tone you use in carrying out the conversation. It's a general rule in human interaction that in most cases emotion trumps reason. Thus, it is essential that the interaction not be perceived as being punitive. Managers who are best at feedback appear low key, even casual in their approach, they see it as an everyday occurrence and they maintain a consistently neutral or positive emotional tone. Doing so precludes a defensive reaction and encourages response. When there is a negative response, such managers do not allow themselves to be engaged in that manner and can usually cool down the interaction by showing interest and asking probing questions. It is never productive to get into verbal fisticuffs with an employee.

The final ingredient of good feedback is the understanding that you are trying to build an effective working relationship with the person. Tom Rath in his charming little book titled *How Full Is Your Bucket?* notes that positive interactions build the trusting relationships that are essential to the productive interaction of people within organizations. The essential principle in this management practice is that respectful behavior builds trust.

Unfortunately, evidence exists that reading this article is not very likely to change behavior. Although the above process appears elementary, its skilled practice requires a good deal of tacit knowledge that can only be learned through experience.

If you want to improve the feedback skills of your managers, consider the following simple but effective approach. Bring a small number (seven is ideal and 12 is too many) of them together for a series of weekly skill-building meetings. Introduce the principles and have the participants practice with each other in scenarios they create based on their experience.

Break them into triads and make sure they get a lot of feedback on their performance and that the group does an overall debriefing of the process. Then have them identify their direct reports into high, average and low performers. Ask them to identify two or three average performers and provide feedback to them at least twice during the week. At the next meeting debrief and coach them, gradually adding all their employees to the mix, saving the low performers for last, as these will be more difficult.

A process like this not only uses the key principles but also actively engages each manager with her people, provides coaching and gradually builds a mutual support group. There are many details, but these ingredients define the core process. The striking outcome is that about the third or fourth week the managers begin to report improved performance with the people who have received feedback as well as higher comfort levels, especially with the more difficult people. Surprise, surprise.

Go To:
KISSing and Chunking: A Magical Method for Better Communications (1.4)
Candor Is a Valuable Trait in Successful Leaders (1.5)
Action-Oriented Style (2.6)

Improving Your Communications through Active Listening

There is hardly anything a person can do that is so respectful and complimentary to another than to seriously and sincerely listen. Yet on a day-to-day basis in the workplace and elsewhere, there is very little evidence of people practicing good listening skills. Consider how often we are either not heard or misunderstood in both our private and work lives. Why?

There seem to be several reasons for poor listening. First, Americans always seem to be in a hurry and the "hurry-up syndrome" precludes taking the time, however brief, to listen to people. Second, most of us have a quite natural tendency to be thinking of our response when others are speaking. This interferes with good listening and we often miss critical elements, make an inappropriate response and inadvertently offend others. How then can we improve our listening skills?

By practicing a simple procedure called "active listening." Although there are many facets to active listening, the essential ingredient is to restate or summarize what the other person has said. This forces us to attend to the content of the message. Such restatements often begin with phrases such as "I understand you to say..." or "Do you mean..." The effect is to slow down the conversation and this markedly improves understanding. This tool can be enhanced by the simple strategy of making eye contact when people are speaking to you. Try the following steps to better listening:

- Show your interest in what the other person has to say.
  - Make eye contact, pay attention
  - Communicate with body language that you're listening (nodding, etc.)
- Ask questions to clarify what you have heard.
- Let the other person know that you understand.
  - Briefly summarize the other person's main points.

Use this tool and you will markedly reduce the tendency of conversations to be people talking at each other. The benefits of effective listening are fourfold.

> # There is hardly anything a person can do that is so respectful and complimentary to another than to seriously and sincerely listen.

1. Receive more information.
2. Show your respect for the views of others.
3. Earn the respect and confidence of others.
4. Save time.

Listening can also be an effective conflict-management tool. When someone initiates a conflict (think of an upset customer or co-worker), they are usually "hot."By skillfully using the above practices, you can begin to cool off the situation and develop an understanding of the person's concerns. Then problem solving can begin. Use the following process to improve listening:

Divide into groups of three and rotate through the three roles:

• Speaker — the person telling a story.
• Listener — the person using the above principles.
• Observer — third party observing and analyzing the interaction.

Work individually to outline a two to five minute story about something at work. The "speaker" then tells the story to the "listener." The "listener" should actively practice the above principles. The observer will watch and listen carefully and make notes. When you are finished, the observer will discuss the interaction with the other two participants using the three bullets to analyze the listening skills.

Then rotate the roles until all three of you have been in each role. When you have finished, discuss all the interactions and be prepared to report your analyses to the full group.

Go To:
KISSing and Chunking: A Magical Method for Better Communications (1.4)
Respectful Behavior (2.4)
Coping with Difficult Situations (5.5)

KISSing and Chunking: A Magical Method for Better Communications

Ever noticed how some people are very effective in both oral and written communications whereas others seem unable to communicate anything clearly?

In 1956, the psychologist George Miller wrote a classic article titled "The Magical Number Seven Plus or Minus Two: Limits On Human Information Processing Capacity." In this article, Miller defined what good communicators intuitively understand: the key to effective communication. People mentally store and retrieve information in "chunks," and the maximum size of a chunk is seven plus/minus two. Thus if you want to have people remember what you say and write, simply follow the "KISS and chunk rule." Keep It Short and Simple and make sure that your chunks do not exceed the magical seven plus/minus two.

This principle is obvious to good communications. If I say or write a small number of things — a "chunk" — you can easily remember and act on them. If, on the other hand, I give you too many bits of data, you will have difficulty remembering them and thus will not be able to act on them. Many managers are ineffective because they "information overload" their colleagues and employees.

Note that large amounts of data can be reduced to smaller chunks and organized hierarchically. There doesn't seem to be any limit to how many chunks a person can store and retrieve if they are thoughtfully organized. The next time you read a newspaper or report or hear a speaker, ask, "What are the 'chunks' in this communication?" Once you identify them, recalling the information will be much easier.

Think about ways to apply these principles. The use of "bullets" in written communications can make letters, memos or reports much more effective. In oral communications, define the chunk of information and organize supporting material around it. While reading memos and reports, look for the "main points" and note them on paper. When in a meeting, look for the important "take-aways." Remember, the ability to chunk is a measure of cognitive efficiency.

Chunking also applies to organizational effectiveness. Using the chunk as a principle to determine organizational levels, functions, departments or divisions markedly reduces complexity and improves effectiveness. Seven plus/minus two is also the optimal size of a committee, team, group, etc. Many otherwise effective groups do not function well because they are too large.

In the case of communication, fewer is better, less is more.

The chunking principle also applies to personal effectiveness. A general rule of management is that effective people and organizations "do a few things well." Focus is an important aspect of high performance. People and organizations that try to do too many things (more than nine) often do none of them well. Peter Drucker often noted that effective managers and executives focus on one to three major issues. In the case of communication and performance, fewer is better.

Practitioners of effective strategic management understand that a handful of powerful issues, priorities and goals is much more likely to be accomplished than a large number. An organization or person with 15 No. 1 priorities really has no No. 1 priority and usually accomplishes little. The next time you communicate, organize, staff or prioritize, use the "magical seven" to enhance people performance.

Go To:
The Power of Information (2.3)
Good Leaders Take Responsibility for Communication (3.9)
The Information Continuum (3.15)

Candor is a Valuable Trait in Successful Leaders

I am not fond of books by retired business leaders, especially autobiographies, as they tend to be biased and self-serving. However, in Jack Welch's *Winning*, his wife, a former *Harvard Business Review* editor, has managed to coax an enormous amount of tacit knowledge out of his experience and onto the printed page. Chapter 2, "Candor: The Biggest Dirty Secret in Business," is particularly worth a discussion.

In earlier segments, we have noted that when you become a supervisor, a manager and finally an executive, peoples' behavior toward you changes, often quite dramatically. People who once were frank with you now begin to "spin." The reasons for this are thought to be complex, but really it often comes down to the "killing the messenger" phenomenon. Almost everyone in an organizational setting has seen what too often happens when someone puts a new idea or a piece of bad news on the table before a person in power. An immediate and powerful negative emotional response is all too often the result. Such a poor demonstration of power can cascade throughout an organization and have a chilling effect on direct, honest communications, particularly upwards. Many years ago I made a career change and left an organization I loved because of a boss who I believed had the philosophy of "never let a good deed go unpunished."

In the book, Welch notes that candor in an organization has three major positive effects. First, it gets people into the conversation, and with more ideas and frank discussions, better decisions are the potent outcome. Second, candor generates speed, and speed in our competitive economy is a powerful competitive advantage. Third, candor cuts costs by eliminating meaningless, non-contributing functions such as pointless meetings and lack of follow-through.

One company I have worked with has a significant division led by a person who seems to be utterly motivated by the need to avoid any, even the most minor, conflict. When presented with any type of negative information she literally leaves the scene and pretends there is no issue. Because she is unwilling to acknowledge any negative issue, she essentially "freezes out" anyone who brings bad news into management discussions.

The major effects of this are two-fold. First, because she is unwilling to

Candor gets people into the conversation, and with more ideas and frank discussions, better decisions result.

acknowledge, albeit manage any negative feedback about her behavior, she literally cannot improve her management skills. It is clear that high-performing managers elicit and use constant feedback from their work environment. This is often the reason that confident, capable managers engage consultants. Often, consultants are the only persons that give them timely, accurate and frank feedback.

The second effect is more organization-wide and is even more pervasive in its results. Because any topic that has a negative connotation to this manager is essentially off limits, a large and ever increasing set of information critical to the success of the business becomes unavailable for open conversation and problem solving. Organizations are quite transparent from the bottom-up. Employees can accurately see manager behavior upward for at least two layers. When a senior manager fails to acknowledge and act on any type of negative information, it causes people to lose confidence in the ability of management to run the business successfully.

The fascinating paradox about this powerful form of negative communication is that most employees report that they would rather work for a manager who is "tough" but acknowledges bad news and acts on it. Clearly employees would prefer to be "hammered" rather than "frozen" if there is follow-through and progress is being made.

Opening an organization to timely, frank and honest communications can be a difficult task for a leader. This is especially the case if there has been a history of punishment for candor as in the above company. It is very clear that "active" sensing systems in organizations work much better than "passive." Skillful "management by walking around" is far superior to the suggestion box (a tool that is thankfully disappearing from the modern workplace). The challenge for the leader is to create situations and opportunities where she invites input and then handles the information in a manner that makes sense to people.

Some years ago, I worked closely with an extraordinary leader who carried out a successful turn-around in a deeply troubled company. He spent much of the first two months visiting with people throughout the organization to develop a clear understanding of what the problems were and what needed to be fixed. When I spoke with people in the organization about these conversations they often responded that what impressed them was that he asked questions. When I pressed them about what kind of questions were asked, they often remarked that the questions were usually very simple but very hard to answer. In carrying out these informal visits throughout the company, this executive constructed a network of reasonable and thoughtful people he could visit with at any time to get a clear sense of the current issues throughout the organization. He had created a powerful tool to sense the organization's immediate performance.

Go To:
One-on-One Feedback is Vital for Your Employees (1.2)
Coaching to Improve Performance (1.6)
Action-Oriented Style (2.6)

Coaching to Improve Performance

People profit from the individual positive attention of another, whether the person is a teacher, parent, colleague or manager. Effective managers take the time to do one-on-one coaching with their direct reports. This time spent with employees usually yields rich results. However, it does require an understanding of the learning process and a level of skill and patience that is learned through practice.

In a 1988 book titled *Zapp* by Bill Byham is a description of the seven stages of an effective coaching process.

1. Explain the purpose and importance of what you are trying to teach. People usually want to know why you are asking them to perform in a particular manner or to develop a specific skill. It is a shame that the ubiquitous question of small children, "why?" is often lost when they grow up. As a manager, you should remember that any instruction or request to another that cannot be succinctly explained needs to be reconsidered. It is perfectly reasonable for people to ask why.

2. Explain the process to be used. Showing people the steps of a process, just as this segment is showing you the steps of the coaching process, helps people to understand the "how" of the process and to formulate a cognitive plan to learn the process. It also forces the manager to revisit the process and consider if it could be improved in some fashion. Perhaps the improvement could result from fewer steps, improved clarity of instructions or even a complete re-building of the process. In each of these cases, remember that simplicity always trumps complexity.

3. Show how it's done. There is compelling evidence that watching someone perform can greatly facilitate learning a skill. It is also of value to mentally rehearse the performance and you should suggest this to the person. This step should be performed in a manner that invites the person to ask questions to clarify their understanding of the task. Beginning at this stage, the generous use of patience will produce improved learning.

4. Observe while the other person practices the process. Immediately after completing the first three steps, have the person engage in the behavior. Let them carry out the entire process, do not interrupt and watch carefully how they are doing.

5. Provide immediate and specific feedback. Giving feedback is another valuable managerial skill and can make or break the coaching interaction. It is important to reinforce good behavior and to identify less-than-satisfactory behavior in a manner that communicates your interest in the person. Being hypercritical is not a good way to begin a coaching relationship. Consider an approach something like this: "That was pretty good, but if you did this (model the behavior here) it would be even better" — so the principle here is coach again and reinforce success.

Almost all people profit from individual positive attention from someone they respect.

---

6. **Express confidence in the person's ability to be successful.** End the session by reiterating the stages of the process, making suggestions on practice to improve performance and expressing your confidence in their ability to accomplish the assignment.

7. **Agree on follow-up actions.** Schedule a follow-on meeting fairly soon to review the performance, continue any coaching as needed and continue to build the working relationship.

This type of structured coaching almost always works unless the manager is unprepared or impatient or if the employee is one of those unusual people who are not interested in learning. If the latter is the case, coaching is an excellent tool to identify this indifference and remove the employee from the workforce before the end of her probationary period.

One tool that managers can make effective use of in coaching is an article appropriate to the situation. This book is a set of article-like segments that cover a variety of real-world topics, and when coaching or giving feedback, the manager can then share the article with the employee to reinforce the one-on-one session. The manager then follows up on this assignment and asks the employee to reflect on what the key ideas of the article were in relation to the issue under discussion.

Here is a triad process to use with a group of managers to markedly improve their skills.

1. First member of the triad develops and carries out an actual coach-

ing session with the second member of the triad from the list of suggested topics. This must be an actual behavior, skill or practice.

2. Third member provides feedback to the coach on process. Rotate, do it, rotate again.

3. On a flipchart: List the topics/behaviors coached and then discuss and list lessons learned.

4. Full group: Round robin discussion of lessons learned.

Go To:
The Basics of an Effective Management Style (1.1)
Harness the Power of Mentoring in Your Business (3.20)
What are the Characteristics of a Great Workplace? (4.6)

1.7

To Improve Productivity, Try Saying Thank You

One of my favorite questions for senior professionals in any field is, "How has this endeavor changed since you first joined it many years ago?"

The question is designed to elicit reflections based on careers sometimes as long as 35 years. Often the responses show great insights and sometimes elucidate how organizations and our larger society are changing.

Recently, a client turned the question back to me by rephrasing it slightly to, "What is the single most important thing you have learned over more than two decades of consulting in a wide variety of organizations?"

What instantly came into my mind was: People in organizations want to be treated respectfully. It then occurred to me, as the optimist I am, that over the course of my career, the practice of management has become more respectful and thus more challenging. It is easy to tell people what to do, but it requires sophistication and skill to build employee commitment to perform in the workplace.

A colleague often notes that you can make people work but you cannot make them work well. My first job, as a laborer in a lead smelter in Montana, taught me that the primary management technique at that time was management by force. All of us were a little bit afraid of the foremen even though they were our neighbors. In today's marketplace, where we value people for their minds, not their muscles, the Gen Xers are teaching us that if we don't treat them well they are gone.

People in organizations want to be treated respectfully.

Rereading one of Peter Drucker's fine articles on management and organizations, I ran across the following statement: "Courtesy is the lubricant that makes organizations work." Wouldn't it be lovely if this statement was posted at the door of every organization and that people would live by it? The statement triggered a train of thought about my best and worst clients. Interestingly, there is an almost one-to-one relationship between how productive an organization is and how respectfully it treats its employees and customers.

If everyone would simply follow this prescription I would be out of work, and clearly I am not. Why not? When I reflect on the circumstances where I was not as courteous or respectful as I should have been, the intervening variable seems to always be that I was not as emotionally grounded at that moment as I should have been. I acted impulsively and thoughtlessly. Simply put, in these situations emotion trumped reason.

This conclusion leads to the literature on emotional intelligence and the idea that emotions are highly contagious. Thus, one of the major behavioral challenges for people, especially managers, in the workplace is to understand their emotions as well as the emotions of others, to understand that some situations set off our emotions involuntarily. These insights guide us to considering how to better manage ourselves.

What better and simpler way to do this than to make a concerted effort to be unfailingly courteous to those we work and live around. For example, over the years I have evolved a personal perception of a male type I refer to as the gentle man, as opposed to gentleman. I have noticed that thoughtful, sensitive women quickly recognize gentle men because of the particularly respectful manner in which they treat women. This type is a rare breed and I only know a handful of such males.

But back to the main point, my mother used to say, somewhat more colorfully, that in life it's not the elephants that get you — it's the ants. Little day-to-day, moment-to-moment irritations and micro-insults can have a corrosive effect in the workplace. The reciprocal is also true: Small courtesies, genuinely shared, can make any situation have a better emotional feel. And amazingly enough all of us know the most powerful of these — thank you and please, but how infrequently we use them. Food for thought.

Go To:
One-on-One Feedback Is Vital for Your Employees (1.2)
Employee Attitude Change: Fishing and Zapping (1.12)
Respectful Behavior (2.4)

1.8

Managing Better Meetings

A theme that often emerges from organizational assessments is that people perceive they are attending too many useless meetings. Employees note that meetings rarely start on time, have any clear purpose and too often dissolve in side conversations or bickering.

As work becomes more complex and requires more communication and cooperation among participants, the importance of effective meetings becomes more critical to organizational productivity. Part of a manager's function is to carry out effective meetings, yet most lack the skills to do so. Here are some simple principles for good meeting management.

An effective meeting must have a leader. Meetings often degenerate because no one has taken responsibility for managing the process of meeting. It is the duty of a leader to take responsibility for managing the process. This means following the "be prepared" motto and assuring that the following conditions exist:

A good meeting must first have a clear purpose. Are we meeting at 9 a.m. on Monday because we have always done so? People prefer to attend meetings that either have clear goals or where the first item on the agenda is to formulate clear goals. If all meeting participants asked the question, "Why are we here?" and no satisfactory answer was apparent, many meetings would immediately discontinue. The development of explicit goals gives direction to any endeavor.

As organizations move to more manager and employee engagement, ineffective meetings become a barrier to productivity.

Meetings need an explicit set of ground rules, principles of how we will behave and treat each other. As meetings are one of the major tools of teams, such expectations, when constructed collaboratively, can greatly enhance the productivity of a meeting. Here is an example of an excellent set of ground rules developed by a team that consists of managers and employees:

• Be/start on time, stay on task and end on time.

• Commit to attend and conduct effective regularly scheduled agenda-driven meetings.

• Be courteous and show respect for others' ideas by letting everyone contribute in turn.

• Solve problems; don't place blame.

It took this team perhaps an hour of discussion to develop these principles. Because they formulated them collaboratively there is a shared commitment to follow them.

Another important element of a successful meeting is an agenda. Once clear goals are formulated, an agenda comes easily. The agenda makes explicit the topics, their order and the time allocated for each. Good agendas rarely have more than five to nine items. A good way to kill a meeting is to make the agenda too long or too complex. In a situation where there have been serious meeting management problems, it is appropriate to assign times to the agenda. It is also important that the agenda include a section that summarizes the results of the meeting and defines work assignments as well as the time and place of the next meeting. Assuring a stable time and place for the meeting will enhance attendance.

The goals, ground rules and agenda provide tools for the leader to manage the meeting process. People respond positively to simple statements such as "we are off task" or "please remember ground rule No. 3" or "it is time to move on to item two." Such gentle reminders can keep a meeting flowing smoothly.

The final conditions for a successful meeting are membership and size. A committee, group or team cannot accomplish its purpose if the appropriate people are not in attendance. Meetings work much better when they have enough people but not too many. In most cases the optimal number is five to nine. Groups above about 10 rarely work together well. Larger groups need an effective sub-committee structure to function well.

Meeting management is a skill that improves when it is based on a set of principles. The most effective method to improve the quality of a meeting is to analyze the meeting's problems and discuss how to resolve them as a group. For example, the leadership role could be rotated so each participant had responsibility for meeting management for an agreed-upon number of meetings. This gets everyone in touch with how difficult it can be to run an effective meeting. Another useful tool is to take several minutes at the end of the meeting and do a round-robin on how the meeting went. The key to better meeting management is to appreciate that meetings need to be managed.

Go To:
Tactical to Strategic (2.8)
SMART Action Plans Help Direct Work Toward Goals (3.8)
Focus on Opportunities and Run Good Meetings (3.12)

1.9

Beware: Change Imposed
Is Change Opposed

But we have always done it this way! How many of you have heard this phrase and what is your emotional reaction to it? Probably "too often" and "not too pleasant."

We live in a workplace of continuous change. Every aspect of jobs and companies is evolving under pressures that include technology, competition and globalization. People, on the other hand, are creatures of habit, and habits can be very hard to change. As an early 20th century psychologist remarked, "Habits are cobwebs that grow into cables."

Those of us who are married know how hard it is to change our cherished patterns of behavior. But if we don't change, both personally and professionally, we are toast. So how can we create a nimble workplace that invites and encourages people to change?

We can think of change management as having four possible steps:

1. Setting the stage by telling stories about change.

2. Explaining how we are changing and why. Defining, as far as possible, the upcoming change.

3. Examining the opportunities and threats that can result from this change.

4. Inviting people into the change process.

Step one involves sharing what might be called "rate of change" stories with your people. This technique provides people with context to understand and frame the changes. Most of us know how powerful stories are, especially when they touch us personally. All of us know stories that contrast people and companies who seized an opportunity and were successful versus those who did not and crashed and burned.

One of my favorites is how a Japanese company named Seiko took most of the watch and clock market from the Swiss in a few short years with a technology that the Swiss matchmakers invented. Or the one about a warehouse full of slide rules made obsolete by handheld calculators.

There are also very personal stories about people who encountered challenges in their lives and used this event to lever themselves to a new and better life. One of my favorites is about an employee who was fired by one of my early clients and used his severance and initiative to start what is today a multimillion-dollar business.

Step two is to explain why the change is taking place. For example, virtually everyone these days has experienced the less-than-joyful effects of an IT upgrade. Some of this pain can be minimized if people understand the why and the how, and there is an ongoing effort to inform them of the progress of the project. Remember, in organizations, good information drives out bad information. But when people don't have information they tend to gossip, and some gossip very negatively and creatively. Set up some kind of informal or formal feedback mechanism so employees do not inadvertently contribute negatively to the grapevine.

Those of us who are married know how hard it is to change our cherished patterns of behavior.

Step three is not only a tool to enhance understanding but can reduce the worry by clarifying what may result. When we examine the negatives that can result from change they then become concrete. This helps to make them less threatening because they are knowable. The most powerful fears result from ignorance.

Catastrophic uncertainty is extremely corrosive to peoples' attitudes. At this point, you can also predict that unexpected events will happen and this can teach people that even when we do our homework carefully, it is hard to predict the future.

Step four is the application of an important management philosophy: Whenever possible, do things with people, not to them. Trying as much as possible to get ownership or buy-in to a change can go a long ways to minimizing resistance. Often in failed change efforts, the analysis might read: a good idea badly done. And most often the critical omission was a failure to bring enough people into the process, even if in only a small way.

Change imposed is change opposed. This is a simple principle but hard to practice, especially when we are in a hurry, and we are always in a hurry. This is the time in organizations where leadership clearly trumps management. Peter Drucker once said, "Managers do things right, but leaders do the right thing."

Go To:
Tactical to Strategic (2.8)
SMART Action Plans Help Direct Work Toward Goals (3.8)
Focus on Opportunities and Run Good Meetings (3.12)

1.10

Making Performance Appraisal Work

Employee surveys usually find that one of workers' major concerns is the lack of feedback — positive and negative — they receive from their immediate supervisor. Yet, most companies have some type of formal performance-appraisal system. What is the explanation for this inconsistency?

First, employees usually are talking about feedback on a frequent or day-to-day basis. In most companies, this usually doesn't happen often enough. The need for such feedback is acute. How can I do better if no one tells me how I'm doing now? *The One-Minute Manager* still sells well after all these years and is a testament to the need for feedback. It is a book that can be reduced to a single sentence: Give your employees timely, accurate feedback about their performance. It also contains a single important, but unspoken message: Give feedback in a neutral or positive tone. No hollering, screaming, threatening, sarcasm or swearing, please.

To become a better supervisor, try this simple trick. Make a list of all your employees and see to it that you speak to them each day about their performance. Opening these conversations with a question is an invitation for them to participate and transmits that you care. If you haven't been doing this they will think you are a little strange at first, but you will be surprised at the improvement in your working relationships and eventually in their performance.

As for formal performance-appraisal systems - why don't they work

An excellent appraisal is a frank and open discussion about the person's professional development. It is not a type of progressive discipline.

better? Why do managers and employees consider them a hassle? One major source of this hassle is a fundamental misunderstanding about the purpose of appraisal.

An excellent appraisal is a frank and open discussion about the person's professional development. It is not a type of progressive discipline. Progressive discipline is a remediation tool used when a person is under-performing and needs to change. This tool consists of a series of stages that become less collaborative and more authoritarian if the employee fails to show improvement. Extensive documentation is an integral part of this process because it can lead to termination of employment. It is very important to never use appraisal as a tool for employee discipline. Progressive discipline, with lots of consultation from your boss and the HR department, is the tool of choice for the non-performer.

Another flaw of appraisals is that when managers get around to doing them they usually rate everybody about the same, fairly positively. This is an error that often comes back to haunt managers when they want to discipline an employee and are faced with a paper trail that says that the employee has been doing satisfactory work.

Yet a third problem with appraisals is that the supervisor often saves up problems and then shares them at review time. This technique is known as "gunny-sacking" and the name fits. There is little purpose to sharing a problem that is months old. Just what can an employee do about something that happened some time ago? Please remember: Bad news doesn't age well.

How can you solve the problem of changing the performance evaluation from an experience we tend to avoid to one that can have positive effects on employee performance and improve working relationships?

A good strategy is to involve the employee early so he or she feels part of the process. A way to do this is to meet with the employee several days before the scheduled appraisal and ask him to fill out a copy of the

appraisal on himself. Four recommended questions are:
— What have you accomplished this year? Make your best case for yourself.
— What haven't you accomplished this year? Why?
— What do you want to accomplish next year? Be explicit about your goals.
— How can I help you?

Then you both do the appraisal form and at the meeting exchange and read the appraisals. You should find that this creates a positive tone and leads to a productive conversation. Obviously this approach is not appropriate for a poorly performing employee. The manager does a final appraisal incorporating the key information that resulted from the interchange. The focus of this type of appraisal should be on future development of performance, not a litany of past mistakes. Use this as an opportunity to grow better employees.

Go To:
One-on-One Feedback Is Vital for Your Employees (1.2)
Engagement and Decision Making (2.5)
It's Important to Give Employees Vital Information (3.10)

1.11

Bottom-Up and 360° Feedback

In an earlier segment, I examined how important one-on-one feedback is in improving the performance of employees, the core elements of an effective feedback process and briefly reviewed a process for building feedback skills in managers.

In recent years, there has been a trend toward broadening the scope of the feedback process to include input not just from an employee's manager but also to include her/his peers, and for persons in a managerial role, his/her direct reports. My observation is that technology-driven companies seem to be more comfortable and successful with this approach.

It is a fair generalization to note that the post-boomer generations, Gen X and Millennials, are more accustomed to and comfortable with feedback. This is probably a positive side effect of the self-esteem movement that has shaped child raising and teaching practices for these groups. For a longer discussion, ask me about the negative side effects of the self-esteem movement or just talk to a manager who hires a wide range of entry-level employees. The terms "unrealistic expectations" and "entitlement" will come up a lot. Unconditional positive feedback is nonsense; we learn from our mistakes.

The most general approach is labeled the 360-degree assessment where input is elicited from the person's manager, peers and direct reports. When carried out effectively, this essentially develops a picture of employee performance from below, sideways and above. In organizations that are trying to improve communication and cooperation in all three directions, this can be a useful tool. Most organizations do not do a full 360-degree review because of the expense and complexity involved, but instead do one or a combination of these assessment techniques.

Earlier, we limited ourselves to the more traditional top-down review by managers. This is most useful for the purpose of day-to-day feedback and scheduled reviews of the person's professional development.

The bottom-up review of managers is most useful as an assessment and measurement tool in coaching a manager to improve her/his managerial skill level. The simplest format for eliciting this data is to send the assessment, with an appropriate cover letter, to each direct report. This note should come from the manager in question and his or her boss. A single sheet with a statement such as "For Angie to improve her managerial performance she should do: More, Same, Less." The three adjectives should be appropriately spaced down the page. The survey should be returned to the senior manager or consultant using a process that provides anonymity.

In recent years, there has been a trend toward broadening the scope of the feedback process to include peers and direct reports.

The resulting narrative information is transcribed to further assure anonymity and then the content is analyzed. The result is a Pareto chart that groups into the expected three to five chunks, gives an accurate profile of the manager's development issues and thus serves as a valuable coaching tool. I often have worked with clients whose self-confidence was such that they shared the information with the participants, usually in a group, and then discussed the developmental plan that came out of the process. This sets the stage to invite the participants into an ongoing feedback mechanism that can raise the manager's skill level very rapidly.

A useful question to ask managers is, "Who are your key internal customers?" The answer to this question is usually a small set of people in lateral positions who make systems and processes work across boundaries (i.e. departments, units, divisions).

In situations where peer-to-peer communication and cooperation is critical to the accomplishment of work, the sideways portion of the 360-degree review can be very useful. The manager identifies her key internal customers and then uses a similar process to invite explicit change suggestions from them. The wording of the driver statement is altered to say "For us to…" In this case, anonymity and the use of a group process for feedback is not indicated. Rather, the manager can have a one-on-one with each of her direct reports and the dyad can then review the resulting Paretos, discuss the information and develop mutual explicit expectations and/or goals to enhance performance.

A slightly different version of this process can be carried out between units, departments or divisions, subject to the usual size limitations, that are having boundary issues. This inter-departmental tool speaks directly to William Deming's observation that most quality problems happen at organizational boundaries. Thus it can be used effectively without the burden of extensive pre-training that often burdens quality initiatives. The consultant or internal coordinator provides the quality tools to the group as immediately needed. This is a powerful method to quickly help people acquire the tacit knowledge they need to succeed in a change effort.

The beauty of the application of parts of the 360-degree process is that this is respectful of peoples' time, uses the very processes that are imparted and involves participants in the change process immediately by inviting their active participation. One concern that is sometimes voiced is that an anonymous process may elicit thoughtless or cruel comments. My experience is that when the process is thoughtfully organized such that people realize the information will be shared with them in some format, this effectively precludes such behavior. People do not want to see their ugly comments, even if anonymous, shared in some open format.

This is yet another piece of evidence for the power of transparency in organizations. These tools also transform traditional one-on-one feedback from individual competence building to organizational development.

Go To:
One-on-One Feedback Is Vital for Your Employees (1.2)
Making Performance Appraisal Work (1.10)
Engagement and Decision Making (2.5)

1.12

Employee Attitude Change: Fishing and Zapping

How many psychologists does it take to change a light bulb? One, but the light bulb must want to change.

In the organization-development consulting business we are all too often confronted with long-term employees, often in bargaining units, that have an "attitude." The attitude consists of complaining, whining, pointing out how bad management is, manipulating their co-workers to act in ways that are not in anyone's best interests, doing rather low-quality or no work and generally avoiding responsibility for their actions. In sensing sessions, employees often complain volubly about such co-workers.

We often refer to this constellation of behaviors, emotions and perceptions as the "entitlement mentality." These patterns of behavior are often deeply embedded in the organization and usually have their origins long before the current managers arrived on the scene. In interviews, insightful longer-term employees often say it was this way when they were hired 30-plus years ago. Often, managers have contributed to this situation by using inappropriate tactics to survive. A couple of these tactics are avoiding and smoothing. In some managers these maladaptive tactics are as embedded as in the troubled employees.

If an organization has a large enough proportion of such people, they constitute a major barrier to improving the organization's functioning. As in the opening quip, it is evident that behavior change only happens when people choose to change. It is also evident that punitive measures, such as progressive discipline, foster sympathy for such people, as in "Didn't I tell you how bad management is?" In addition, the problem of enlisting managers in the change process who have been getting by for many years can be substantial. Many will talk the talk but not walk the walk, and such behavior is a credibility buster.

How can we create a non-threatening context in companies that invites people to change? In the past several years, two brief books have come on the scene that offer an opportunity to do so. These are *Zapp!* and *Fish!* Both are essentially parables about organizational change.

Zapp! tells its story in an industrial setting whereas in *Fish!* the setting is

How many psychologists does it take to change a light bulb? One, but the light bulb must want to change.

a service support center. Each story is of a toxic work environment that is changed by a leader who offers hope by openly recognizing the issues and then inviting employees to help change them to create a better working environment. This is done in a trial-and-error approach where no one is punished and everyone can contribute if they choose. Critical to the change process, each book offers a set of core principles about how to work together. Interestingly, each defines four core principles.

I have consulted in several work settings where one or the other of these books has been a powerful lever for improvement in the culture. The necessary conditions for this to work are that supervisors and key employees must take up the principles and commit to using them in their everyday work settings. Where this happens with the support of senior management, experience shows that a large proportion of employees willingly join in and the culture of the workplace begins to change for the better.

In the one instance of this happening, the senior on-site manager essentially snubbed the book but a key supervisor and a group of employees used it to change the environment rapidly and radically. As the consultant on-site and with the support of senior managers, I was able to assist them with tools to ensure the change was real and long lasting.

Go To:
Engagement and Decision Making (2.5)
What Is Your Attitude Toward Work? (4.2)
If You See a Bathroom, Use it! (5.2)
Surviving and Thriving in Changing Environments (5.3)

Managing Troubled and Troublesome Employees

A few difficult employees can create big problems for management. Some workers produce mayhem on the job. They waste time, waste company money, irritate fellow workers, frustrate managers, destroy morale and present a bad image of the company to customers. Other employees lag in performance while dealing with a difficult personal problem, yet create little adversity for the rest of the company.

Problem employees may be divided into two categories: The troubled employee and the troublesome employee. A troubled employee does not function as well as is needed in the workplace. Everyone at some time will become a troubled employee. Family problems, over-promotion, drug abuse, ill health or inadequate skills are just a few of the problems that can cause an employee who normally functions well to fall below usual competence levels.

Troubled employees can benefit from thoughtful, sensitive management. Fellow employees usually are sympathetic toward troubled workers. They watch closely how management treats troubled employees because they know some day they may face problems, too.

Troublesome employees, on the other hand, disrupt the entire workplace. They wreak havoc. Their fellow employees often dislike them. Many troublesome employees have common characteristics: anger, cynicism, unrelenting complaining and ducking responsibility. They walk around with a chip on their shoulder; any little thing sets them off. They chew up time and grind people down. They are generally disliked by their co-workers and they often contribute to a toxic workplace.

The distinction between these two types is important if you are a manager. How you treat these people will send very different kinds of messages to your employees. For example, I have personally observed informal celebrations by employees after a troublesome person was terminated.

Obviously, employee performance issues can be very complex. Here are some issues to consider as you approach such problems.

First, you must define the problem, focusing on specific behaviors. Explain to the employee what behaviors are inappropriate and appropriate.

Troublesome employees have common characteristics: anger, cynicism, unrelenting complaining and ducking responsibility.

For example: "I noticed you have been more than 40 minutes late for work four days in a row." That approach works better than saying: "You don't have the right attitude at work." Focus on behavior and help the employee change. Try to create a context where the employee will discuss issues with you. Make sure you fully understand the situation. The difficulty with some problem solving is that people don't learn what the problem is before hurrying to a solution.

Second, find out why it is happening. This may be difficult. Sometimes the problem employee doesn't know the underlying cause of the problem. At other times, learning the reason can lead to an obvious solution. Perhaps the worker who has been late doesn't have a behavior problem at all. Maybe the employee had to hurriedly find a new babysitter who provides different service hours.

Third, the manager must decide who should be involved in the decision-making process regarding an employee. Bringing in other management people, the HR department or, in serious cases, an attorney, mental health professional or the police, may be advisable for additional insight and resources. Many larger companies have employee-assistance programs and they can be very effective.

Fourth, remember that management chooses the time and place to talk with an employee. Never confront problem employees in front of their co-workers. Place a cool-down time between a confrontation and further discussion of an issue. If a troublesome person confronts you in a public situation, suggest that you are busy and will meet them in your office later in the day. When and where to deal with a problem is an advantage that management often throws away. Remember, even with the most difficult person, it is important to treat them respectfully and try to maintain their dignity.

Fifth, discuss possible alternatives for solving the particular problem with the employee. Remember that troubled employees are simply in need of help. The manager who is compassionate and assists the troubled employee builds goodwill among the entire workforce. However, if an employee is troublesome, a harder approach is appropriate. First, know your disciplinary policies cold; you can be sure the troublesome employee will. Progressive discipline could lead to a brief suspension, followed by dismissal if the behavior does not improve. This outcome will probably be best for everyone in the long run. When troublesome employees leave, morale throughout the workplace improves.

Finally, remember as a manager your responsibility is to act in the best interests of the company and within this context build employee performance. In all these cases thoughtful planning trumps impulsive action.

Go To:
One-on-One Feedback Is Vital for Your Employees (1.2)
Courage: Managers into Leaders (2.9)
Values of the Ethical Manager (2.12)

1.14

Using Skip-Level Meetings to Sense the Organization

I often discuss how providing focused, positive feedback to people can serve as a method to begin to open up an organization and invite people to make suggestions and recommendations. It is clear that the best listening or sensing systems are those that actively invite people to share their perceptions and ideas. Passive systems often invite complaining and whining.

A tool that I have seen several managers use to improve listening in their organizations is the "skip-level meeting" or "sensing session." In a typical use of this tool, a senior manager randomly invites nine to 11 employees from throughout the company to have breakfast with her. The manager uses this as an opportunity to get to know employees and "sense" the organization. If the manager is an effective listener and not a

When this tool is applied thoughtfully and skillfully, it is an excellent source of information about employees' concerns.

talker, she will develop an excellent set of impressions about the concerns of employees.

Such a meeting is a valuable tool to keep in touch with the organization. However, this is a tool that is easily misused and care must be taken that this does not happen. Here is a set of principles for the implementation of skip-level meetings.

• Such a process should be planned with the input of the managers in the organization who will essentially be bypassed. The intention of this tool is to sense the organization, not destroy trust within the management structure. Managers will be uncomfortable with this tool until they are assured about its purpose and have input into its design.

• A commitment must be made that the senior manager will not make decisions during such meetings and thereby undercut the management structure. To do so is the worst kind of sub-optimal management practice.

• Everyone must understand that the purpose of the meetings is for the senior manager to reach past levels in the organization and develop informal inputs to sense the organization. This is not a tool to trap or evaluate his or her direct reports.

• The manager who carries out such meetings must have good listening skills. Employees who spend the whole session being lectured report that it is a major turn-off. Striking a balance between listening and talking is a key issue for the manager. Employee participation, elicited by the use of wise questions, is almost always better.

• Care must be taken to avoid the appearance of favoritism in the selection of the persons. Such perceived favoritism will generate distrust of the process.

• The manager must establish ground rules about what and how information she elicits from the meetings will be handled. These ground rules must be shared with appropriate constituents. It is important to avoid the possibility of the appearance of a witch hunt.

When this tool is applied thoughtfully and skillfully, it is an excellent source of information about employees' concerns and often can identify and solve problems, especially communications problems. The reaction of employees is uniformly positive. When they understand the ground rules, they appreciate that the big boss is willing to spend some valuable time to listen to their views. This is one of those active communications strategies that forces managers and employees to rethink some old rules about how communication takes place in the organization.

Go To:
Improving Your Communications through Active Listening (1.3)
Managing Better Meetings (1.8)
Respectful Behavior (2.4)

1.15

Optimizing Your In-House Training Programs

There are three issues that are easy to get people committed to work on: Safety, training and quality. No one wants to work in an unsafe workplace; people want to work smarter because it is personally satisfying and assures their job security and people want to do a good job. The worst thing you can do to your people is put them in situations where they are forced to build poor products or deliver bad services.

The major issue in the development and application of training in organizations is how to increase the likelihood that the concepts and behaviors introduced will be applied in the workplace. Here are the key variables that influence the transfer of training.

Executives communicate their priorities to their managers through their behavior. Training is most effective where senior managers demonstrate their belief in the concepts and practices. The most effective application of training happens when executives are actively involved in the planning and implementation of the training. The least effective are when training becomes "just another human resource program." The heavier the involvement of senior managers in the training, the greater the impact in the company. It is difficult for seminar instructors to field the question "Why aren't our senior managers participating if they think this is so important?"

Training is most effective when it fits the organization's operating style and goals. The more tailored training is, the more impact it will have in the organization. Some type of assessment process is usually necessary as a basis for planning training. My favored approach is a series of interviews or sensing sessions with a carefully chosen sample of employees or managers. This results in recommendations that are developmentally appropriate to the company's current state of functioning. For example, a company recently asked for an assessment of its readiness for team building. The results of the study indicated that at this time other types of training would be more appropriate and effective.

Training is most effective when it fits the organization's operating style and goals.

The less didactic and the more participative the training, the more effective it becomes. Efforts to involve people in discussions, case studies, practice sessions, small-group problem solving, homework, supplemental readings with discussion, etc., will markedly enhance the transfer to the workplace. The best instance of this principle is training programs where the problem solving, goal setting and other activities are directly related to real everyday workplace issues.

The principles of engagement apply very well to the development and implementation of training. Any efforts (interviews, surveys, task groups, etc.) to involve participants in the development of the training will reap major benefits from a sense of ownership. Sometimes in a series of seminars it is possible to actively involve the participants in negotiating how to apply the principles back at work, design the content for the next seminar and define the needs for future training.

The logistics of training (location, size, duration, amenities, composition of the group, etc.) is highly related to its effectiveness. For example, the typical method of determining who will participate is to choose a time and invite people. This approach disregards the fact that carefully tailoring the group can have major positive effects if there is a clear set of goals (i.e. improve interdepartmental communication).

The credibility and skill of the instructor is another key factor. There are two things to look for here. The first is how well the seminar leader understands your business. This is related to how much effort you are willing to invest to assure that this is the case. The second factor, the relative skill of the instructor, is related to the first. The ability to facilitate effective participation is closely related to an understanding of the business and its people.

Internal training is a powerful tool for improving the functioning of organizations. Experience demonstrates that the more attention companies pay to the above variables, the more impact the training will have. I have worked in companies where the training had major effects on the improved performance of managers and employees and thus productivity. I have observed training programs in companies where they had little or no positive effect because of inattentiveness to the above variables.

On a per-person basis, internal training is extremely cost effective. It eliminates transportation costs, it can reach large numbers of persons, everyone receives the same message and it can be well fitted to the developmental needs and goals of the organization. Making this process effective requires significant investment of resources in planning and development.

Go To:
Managing Better Meetings (1.8),
Employee Attitude Change: Fishing and Zapping (1.12)
Engagement and Decision Making (2.5)

Why Most Employee-Recognition Programs Don't Work

I once did a series of employee and supervisor sensing session groups in a large company. The purpose of these groups was to draw a picture of the training needs of managers in the organization and use this information to build a highly focused management-development program. However, to my surprise, one major finding of the groups was that employees and supervisors did not like or appreciate the company's employee-recognition program. This was the perception of every participant in the groups.

Such a finding is not uncommon in companies with recognition programs. Why is it that many programs, designed with the best intentions, turn out to be a turn-off to employees? The answer to this question is of value to you if your program is not having the effects you anticipated or you are considering implementing such a program.

There seem to be three major reasons that such programs do not work well:

1. Programs are often developed and implemented top-down in the organization. The cited program was actually purchased from an outside source. Employees perceive such top-down programs as yet another example of top management's paternalism — doing it to us not with us. Many employees described the program as condescending, yet reported that positive feedback is very important to them.

2. Too often employee recognition is a public affair. Is it not true that for it to be effective there must be a public display of appreciation? No. Many, if not most, employees are embarrassed at being singled out for recognition, and such recognition can often cause hard feeling among employees, especially if they feel that they were slighted and the award was undeserved.

3. As we move to management philosophies that emphasize teamwork, it is probably not appropriate to recognize individual accomplishment in public. In an era when we are trying to foster cooperation, the recognition of individuals may foster destructive competition.

How then can one design and carry out an effective employee-recognition program? The answer is really quite simple — ask the employees to do it. Set up an employee-recognition task force and invite employee participation. Invite a sample of seven to nine volunteer employees that represent

Assessments in companies often find that employees and supervisors did not like or appreciate the company employee-recognition program.

all parts of the organization and consider including one first-line supervisor. Have a senior manager, vice president level, champion the group and empower them to design a program as a proposal to senior management. Then give them the time and resources to do the job. Keep in mind that the membership of this group should be updated in a systematic manner to assure new ideas and to avoid the group becoming dysfunctional.

Successful programs:

1. Are usually designed with extensive employee input and guidance from key managers and sometimes are operated by employees with management oversight. Beware of senior managers who "know what's best for people." They are often wrong and employees perceive such condescension very negatively.

2. Tend to celebrate the success of groups such as departments, teams, or operating units working together, not individuals. Individual recognition is important, but it is best done privately and the grapevine then communicates the recognition.

3. Benefit from the skills of an inside or outside consultant to help manage the process of getting employees involved and assure that the process does not go out of control.

4. Are dynamic. By this I mean that successful recognition programs are constantly changing to avoid or preclude the boredom or satiation effect.

If you are designing or rebuilding a program, consider these points. Attention to them can improve morale and avoid creating a source of complaining.

Go To:
To Improve Productivity, Try Saying Thank You (1.7)
Managing Better Meetings (1.8)
Engagement and Decision Making (2.5)

Driving Quality Improvements with the Internal Customer Model

Perhaps the most powerful model to improve quality is one that focuses on the interdependency of jobs by using the concept of the "internal customer."

If people understand they have customers within the organization, this allows them to examine how they help and hinder inter-related work. Many organizations are obtaining significant productivity and quality gains by bringing groups of employees and managers together to define and analyze their respective jobs and how they affect each other. This often begins with an in-depth analysis of each person's job. Such a discussion usually reveals that most people do not fully understand or appreciate the roles and contributions of their co-workers. The internal customer analysis often begins by using a message exchange driven by the following statements: Here is what you do that helps; hinders; would help more.

The answers to these questions produce a conversation that results in a better understanding of the process of work and quickly identifies and addresses patterns that either assist or hinder others in the accomplishment of their tasks.

When this process is carried out in a skilled fashion within a work group, it quickly identifies, and with the commitment from management, begins to address, a wide range of miscommunications and misunderstandings that cause problems when people have to work together to accomplish tasks. It is interesting that people initially focus on developing smoother processes with their co-workers and then quickly move to identifying organizational barriers to productive work. At this point, a supportive manager or consultant with a clear mandate from senior management is needed to assist in engaging other work units or departments in the process.

We know that sub-optimization, the tendency to do the job in a manner that hinders the work of others, has its most negative effects when companies have departments that behave like vertical silos where there is little cross-communication at the levels where work gets done. In contrast, research on productive and innovative organizations shows that they have excellent lateral communications, especially across boundaries such as

> # The most powerful model to improve quality is one that focuses on the interdependency of jobs by using the concept of the 'internal customer.'

departments. The process of involving employees in analyzing how their jobs interact, the internal customer model, is a fundamental method for addressing the lateral communication and cooperation issue. Where it is applied with attention to involving employees, it produces impressive gains in quality and productivity.

Go To:
Engagement and Decision Making (2.5)
Understanding the Job as a Social Contract (4.7)
Skills Needed for the Job Can Change the Employment Landscape (4.8)
Aid Understanding by Defining the Job as a Social Role (4.9)

Unit 2:
Management Principles

This unit is designed to introduce and discuss a number of principles that often seem to be lacking in management textbooks. These are the foundation principles that are often assumed and thus ignored or forgotten in serious discussions of management. This core set of beliefs, supported by experience, should be the basic philosophy you operate from as a manager.

If management is a principle-driven art, then it is necessary to have a working knowledge of these basic principles.

This unit has three parts:
Nine segments that discuss some of the implicit, unspoken principles effective managers learn by trial and error or by the fortunate luck of having a good mentor. They are organized in a logical sequence and can be paired to support segments about practices from unit 1. These are characteristics that I have observed effective managers use on the job.

1. Organizations and Management
2. Managing: What Are Your Expectations?
3. The Power of Information
4. Respectful Behavior
5. Engagement and Decision Making
6. Action-Oriented Style
7. Principles vs. Rules
8. Tactical to Strategic
9. Courage: Managers into Leaders

Three very important segments on ethical behavior.
10. Why Ethical Behavior Is Profitable
11. How Managers Fail
12. Values of the Ethical Manager

A segment that summarizes what predicts managerial success. If you are growing and promoting managers, this topic is extremely worthwhile.
13. What Predicts Managerial Success

Organizations and Management

The modern organization is a product of the industrial revolution. Before then, the only large organizations were armies.

Three men often are credited with creating the modern industrial organization: Henry Ford for mass production, Samuel Taylor for "scientific management" — the idea of structuring jobs as tasks — and Alfred Sloan, who created the first modern corporation, General Motors, by buying and successfully integrating many small motorcar companies.

Organizations are important because they are how we structure environments to get complex work done on a large scale. The typical hierarchical organization does some things very well, but its bureaucratic structure is inherently resistant to change, and the pace of change is accelerating. This rapid economic evolution has forced traditional organizations to rethink their basic structures. However, organizations must be hierarchical because it is the most efficient method of allocating and managing responsibility and authority that anyone has ever conceived. Misguided change initiatives such as "self-directed work teams" have demonstrated that a chain of responsibility is necessary.

The development of organizations drove the creation of management. The initial model for management was the army, primarily because this structure was the only model available at that time and most of the work of organizations was manual. Since Sloan wrote his classic book, *My Years at General Motors*, in 1963, management has evolved relatively slowly. Many, if not most organizations, are run in an all-too-often less than benevolent top-down fashion. This is not surprising because a general trend of the past 100 years is that industrial and scientific advances have outpaced social and cultural advances.

Peter Drucker stimulated serious thinking about management with his 1945 book, *The Practice of Management*. His insightful and lucid analyses of this field continued throughout his life. Perhaps Drucker's most important contribution was the definition of the knowledge worker, one who works primarily with information or one who develops and uses knowledge in the workplace. Drucker stated that such workers could only be effectively managed with trust, not by force. This is an important concept as we now are firmly embedded in the information economy. One

> ## 'The ultimate product of an effective business is a satisfied customer. Managing this is a principle-driven art.'
>
> ### - PETER DRUCKER

only has to review which jobs are being created and destroyed in first-world economies to see the shift of work from manual to mental. This change presents tremendous challenges to traditional management practice and moves it from the realm of telling people what to do, something two year olds can do well, to building commitment to a common goal.

Drucker notes that the fundamental task of management is to make people capable of joint performance by giving them common goals, common values, the right structure and the ongoing training and development they need to perform and to respond to change. One of management's functions is make peoples' strengths effective and their weaknesses irrelevant. To accomplish this, every enterprise requires simple, clear and unifying objectives and common values.

Information-driven organizations must be built on communication and individual responsibility. Each member of the organization needs to understand what she aims to accomplish and must understand how her individual performance interacts with and affects her colleagues. This clarity of shared expectations is essential to the accomplishment of the organization's purpose.

The ultimate product of an effective business is a satisfied customer. It is the responsibility of managers to engage in practices that result in products, services and information that satisfy customers. How managers do this is a principle-driven art.

Go To:
The Basics of an Effective Management Style (1.1)
Leadership Is an Important Organizational Performance Driver (3.1)
What Are the Characteristics of a Great Workplace? (4.6)

Managing: What Are Your Expectations?

Continuing with our discussion of management, let's review how a person's mindset, attitudes and expectations are a measure of how well they practice the art of management. Then consider three self-questions that measure a set of beliefs that influence how well people manage.

There is compelling evidence that our expectations drive our behavior, often by creating self-fulfilling prophecies. This means that people often act in a fashion that makes their expectations, particularly about others, come to pass. Recently I had a conversation with a senior vice president in an organization where he described in some detail how a high-performance employee was treated so disrespectfully by his manager that the employee abruptly quit. His question to me was: How can such mean-spirited people become so senior and thus so powerful in organizations?

There is no single answer to this question, but I suggested that the manager in question didn't realize how disrespectfully he treated his direct reports. Rather, he had a set of beliefs about his people that we didn't share. Just what those beliefs are would be interesting to know, but it's unlikely that such a manager has even thought about the question.

Having worked with many effective managers over the past couple of decades, it seems to me that most of them have a set of expectations about people that are mostly encapsulated in the following three major beliefs. Please remember that a belief is a combination of thoughts and feelings. Consider these beliefs and reflect upon your own.

First, **excellent managers believe that people are smart.** These managers treat their employees as if they are capable of intelligent thought and action. Some of the indicators of this belief are a willingness to listen to others' ideas, respect for their experience, the skill to work patiently with people to develop goals and a willingness to provide their direct reports with timely, accurate feedback. What this really means is such managers treat their direct reports as if they are fully functioning, mature adults. Almost everyone responds to this type of treatment in a rather positive fashion. This belief and its corresponding behaviors also assure that the manager will not be seen as condescending. Of all the infuriating forms of behavior available, "talking down" to people as if they are dummies has to be one of the most insulting. Working for someone who "knows everything" is insufferable because know-it-alls are completely lacking in common sense.

Second is the belief that **most people really want to do a good job.** Most people understand that when they do a good job they feel good about themselves and vice versa, thus people are usually motivated to engage in behaviors that make them feel good. Of course, it is the manager's responsibility to define explicitly the performance that constitutes a good job. One of the most demoralizing things you can do to employees is put them into situations that force them to do poor work.

One of the most demoralizing things you can do to employees is put them into situations that force them to do poor work.

This belief can carry a manager a long way with her direct reports. What we are talking about are many subtle behaviors that communicate to the employee high performance standards. Many managers cannot drive high performance because they don't expect much. Driving high performance has a salutary effect on people because high performance enhances peoples' self-efficacy. Self-efficacy is an accurate self-perception of competency and is what we often call a "can-do" attitude. A manager who expects that people perform very well is on the road to building a very effective and rewarding work place.

Third is an understanding that **most people know what's wrong and they want to fix it.** This expectation flows from the first two and is the core belief for making effective change. Potential clients sometimes ask me to do customer focus groups for them. I often suggest that they do "internal customer" sensing sessions instead. Customers can see the problems but employees see the problems, usually know what is causing them and often have useful ideas about how to address the problems. Most effective quality-improvement programs, customer-service programs, productivity-improvement initiatives, etc., have this belief at their heart.

I came to these principles about expectations through experience.

When I asked manager Z to describe his people and he said they were lazy, worked only for money and didn't help each other out — sure enough, when I assessed that workplace the situation was as he described it. When I asked manager Y the same question and he described his people as motivated, communicative, cooperative and effective in their jobs — sure enough, when I looked at that workplace, those were the behaviors. People are the same everywhere; the only difference is the behavior of the managers.

Sometimes these expectations are so visible and obvious that they are hidden in plain sight. Two current and compelling examples are the descriptions some people use to describe "older workers" and "Gen Xers." I perceive these groups having the capacity to make enormous contributions to the productivity of organizations, but many managers in the workplace do not.

So, what are your core beliefs about the people who work for and with you? Some serious reflection might yield enormous increases in your personal effectiveness as a manager.

Go To:
What Is Your Attitude Toward Work? (4.2)
Improving Your Personal and Professional Productivity (5.1)
Surviving and Thriving in Changing Environments (5.3)

The Power of Information

As we move deeper into a global, information-driven economy the importance of people in organizations increases. No longer can people be assumed to be interchangeable, easily replaceable parts that can be managed basically by force. Peter Drucker, in his seminal article defining the knowledge worker, states that "we can no longer manage with force, we must manage with trust."

How then can the modern manager manage with trust instead of by force? This is the central challenge of the managerial role. Maybe the best way to introduce the topic is by describing what doesn't build trust in organizations. In a previous segment, I described that people want to be treated with respect, to be treated as mature, fully functioning adults. What are the killer characteristics that violate this expectation and become trustbusters in an organization?

The first trustbuster is secrecy. People want to understand what is going on around them — ignorance is not bliss; it is in fact very dangerous in many ways. Some years ago, I read a book entitled *Beating the Street* by Peter Lynch. His first and most important principle was, "Don't use a financial instrument or invest in a product or service you don't understand." After reading the book I changed brokers because I was being pushed to invest in an instrument with which I wasn't comfortable. Shortly after making this change, the market for this particular type of investment collapsed. Who says books cannot save and make you money?

Information is a powerful tool and we manage information with communication. Communication is then a primary tool in the manager's repertoire and managers, particularly executives, must understand that they are communicating all the time through their actions as well as their words. Effective communication is a major challenge and becomes more so as the size of an organization increases. In very small organizations everyone can know almost everything, but as an organization grows the complexity of assuring clear communication increases exponentially. For a simple example of this, think about how good communication can be in a group of five people, but add five more to the group and communication degrades markedly.

So understanding that it is not possible for everyone to know everything, what do people in the workplace need to know to assure that they are well equipped with the appropriate information to do their jobs well? There are three chunks of information people need to know: 1. As much as possible about their jobs, 2. How their jobs fit into the process of accomplishing work and 3. What is the overall nature of the endeavor they are working within, the "big picture?"

Assuring that employees have the right information is the most fundamental element of effective managing.

First, people live in their jobs and to a large extent our jobs define who we are and provide material, emotional and for some spiritual support for our lives. Performance drives self-efficacy and people cannot perform well if they have insufficient information about their jobs. Knowing this then defines who is responsible for holding and expanding this understanding. First and foremost, it's the employee's responsibility to assure she knows as much as possible about the job, but it is also her immediate manager's job to support her in every way possible to fulfill and expand this under-standing. This shared responsibility is no small challenge.

Second, people need to understand how their work contributes to the process that produces a product or service. The easiest way to understand this is to examine the internal customer model. Simply put, who are the people upstream from you that affect your work and who are those down-stream that your behavior affects? Edwards Deming, the Iowan who brought quality to Japan after WWII, noted that most quality problems happen at boundaries and the most fundamental boundaries in organiza-tions are those between people within a process. This understanding is the basis for almost all effective quality-improvement processes. Clearly, man-agers are responsible for communicating this information because it is out of the reach of most employees.

Finally, people want to know the larger context within which their work resides. This is what many people call the big picture. What is the industry like, how is it changing, what is our company's role within it, what is our purpose, what is our vision, where are we heading, etc. This domain of information is clearly the responsibility of the executive and most executives find it very gratifying that most people are keen to know about the larger strategic aspects of the organization.

Knowing these three fundamentals about your workplace is the antithesis of secrecy; being skilled enough to assure that most if not all employees have this information is a fundamental element of effective managing.

Go To:
Candor is a Valuable Trait in Successful Leaders (1.5)
Good Leaders Take Responsibility for Communication (3.9)
The Information Continuum (3.15)

2.4

Respectful Behavior

In the previous segment, it was noted that there are three trustbusters in organizations, and the first of these is secrecy. Communication is the management tool that erases ignorance and the poor performance resulting from the lack of a good knowledge basis for the job.

The second trustbuster in organizations is disrespectful behavior. I once worked with someone who I still describe as a person that when you first met her, you didn't care much for her, but after you got to know her, you really disliked her. What kind of characteristic could trigger such a description? Consistently disrespectful behavior toward others. This person believed that life was a zero-sum game and that for her to win, others must lose. Such a person can have a grievous emotional impact in an organization.

She was certainly an extreme case, and I have not met her like in 20 years. But consider the less-extreme and more-prevalent attitude and

To be an effective manager, first understand yourself and build skills that project realistic optimism, invite people into the process of work and help them to develop their skill sets.

behavior: Who is to blame? This is a pattern of behavior that seems to be driven by a certain kind of reporting in the press — let's find out who did wrong and then assure they are punished. Such a pattern can have a devastating effect in any environment.

I am fond of pointing out that mistakes, what some people consider doing wrong, provide us with a rich base of information to review, analyze and learn from. Mistakes are certainly opportunities for improvement, but if the prevalent view is let's find the culprit and punish, the effects on people and organizational performance are very perverse.

Consider that you are an employee in an organization that has a pattern of identifying and punishing. What would be your strategy to minimize the level of grief to yourself? Well, of course, you would follow the rules exactly, try to do nothing because it is safer and never try anything new because that is dangerous. What do some people say? No good deed goes unpunished. Such a belief comes from experience.

A key element of respectful communication is consistency. I have worked with people who share very different versions of what should be the same information with others. Such people are generally perceived as manipulative, using information selectively to make change without the recipient being aware of the basic agenda. This is the inverse of influence. Influence is using consistent information to make change when the agenda or purpose is open and all are aware of it.

Some years ago, I had the opportunity to visit individually with a handful of managers who were chosen because of their proven ability to work with people effectively. One of my questions was: So, what makes you a well-respected and effective manager? One of the managers thought about this for a couple minutes, a long time for people to be silent in a conversation, and answered, "I try to be the same man every day." I have never forgotten his response and I have seldom seen so much wisdom in so few words.

For several years after, whenever I visited with employees I asked them to describe the poorest manager, and most often the response was, "What mood is he in today?" The importance of consistent, predictable behavior cannot be underestimated, both in managing and in child rearing. Unpredictability makes it impossible for people to adapt successfully.

Imagine for a moment how profound the change when a manager with a more enlightened philosophy takes over. Employees can trust that what they are told is the same story their colleagues are hearing and the level of trust soars in the organization. Now, the words "thank you" and "please" permeate conversations and mistakes are framed as learning opportunities that are jointly owned. Problem solving replaces blaming, communications immediately begin to improve and the workplace becomes more people-friendly and productive.

As a manager, you must understand how you treat people, through your words, actions and emotions, has an effect on their performance and thus on yours. To be an effective manager, first understand yourself and build skills that project realistic optimism, invite people into the process of work and help them to develop their skill sets.

Go To:
To Improve Productivity, Try Saying Thank You (1.7)
What Is Your Attitude Toward Work? (4.2)
Improving Your Personal and Professional Productivity (5.1)

Engagement and Decision Making

"People support what they help create." So said Mary Kay, a woman who put many other women into pink Cadillacs. When I read her book 20 years ago, I was impressed by the pure common sense of her ideas, but that one phrase has always stuck in my head.

It is an axiom that a small group of people acting in concert is smarter than the sum of its members. Conversely, any group of people not acting in concert can be extraordinarily stupid. One challenge for a manager is how to enhance the former and eliminate the latter. The key to this is to have a full repertory of decision-making styles and to be able to use each appropriately.

Analyzing your own decision-making style is key to the growth and development of the effective manager. In general, we can characterize the types of decision making as being on the following continuum:

> Authoritarian
>> Authoritative
>>> Consultative
>>>> Consensual

Authoritarian is the "old" American style: one way, the right way, my way. It has the advantage of being very fast, but at the cost of limiting and usually eliminating any input from others into the decision. This type of decision making is sometimes perceived by employees as capricious and it often upsets them. Authoritarian decision making is most appropriate in emergency or crisis situations where the chain of command is clear, roles are well defined and understood and people are well trained. An example is a group of firefighters at a fire scene or a squad of soldiers in combat.

Authoritative decision making is a softened version of authoritarian. Many effective managers have a primarily authoritative style. They retain control of the decision but explain how and why they made it. Actually, this means using decision making as a method to communicate the "why" of issues to employees, and this approach is usually respected by employees. Almost all formal teaching and learning situations are authoritative. The instructor defines the topic, content, process and leads the class or seminar. This type of decision-making style requires excellent communication skills, and when used respectfully, is a powerful tool.

Consensual is the Japanese way: Let's talk about this until we all agree and then do it. This method maximizes input but it can be terribly slow to reach consensus. It also has another major disadvantage that is related to culture. Japan is a culture where seeking consensus is trained into people. This is not the case in American culture. Often in Americans, who value individuality above all, real consensus is exceedingly difficult to obtain. In practice, Americans will finally agree, but may then go out and do what they please regardless of the decision.

One key to being an effective manager is to have a full repertory of decision-making styles and to be able to use each appropriately.

The best example of a consensual decision process in American culture is the jury; juries are often slow and make very conservative decisions. Also, when the decision is difficult, juries tend to "hang up" and produce no decision. To work in our culture, consensual decision making requires a powerful shared purpose and very group-process skilled participants. Perhaps the strongest argument against this type of decision is that diffusion of responsibility in groups can unwittingly encourage "group think" and lead to foolish or unethical decisions.

What is needed for effective people engagement is a combination of the best aspects of the two opposite styles. Consultative decision making is a process that encourages input, can be accomplished in a timely fashion and maintains a clear executive function. From the employee-supervisor-manager perspective, it is simply stated: Ask me before you decide. Use your people as consultants in the decision process. Many have ideas about how to do it better, but you must ask them.

Consultative decision making maintains the executive function (i.e. "The buck stops here") and at the same time solicits input. Please remember, people support what they help create. Encouraging input gives people some ownership of the decision by making them participants in the process. This is a style of management where you do things with people, not to them.

It should be noted that many managers use a version of consultative management that appears progressive in practice but is perverse in effect. This is soliciting input from employees and then habitually disregarding the information. Employees manage to figure out rather rapidly what is happening and the effects are trust busting. It is more honest and effective to practice direct authoritative decision making than to ask for input and then always disregard it, creating the fiction, but not the fact, of employee involvement. I have seen many managers inadvertently stumble into this mistake, and its effects are negative because employees perceive they are being manipulated.

Consultative decision making also requires a more people-skilled manager. If you create a work climate where people will actively participate, much of what you learn you will not want to hear, though you need to hear it. It takes a very skilled person not to become defensive and overreact to what they might perceive as attacks on their good works. Such management also requires more time. However, the commitment that it builds in employees is demonstrated in improved productivity, an increased capacity to deal with change and a much more positive organizational climate.

The challenge of being an effective manager is not just having all these decision-making styles in your repertory, but knowing when and how to use them. Clearly, there are situations where each of these styles is most appropriate and will produce the best results. The question I ask myself is, "Do I have the appropriate people involved in the decision?" Some decisions require no input or commitment, whereas other decisions are critically dependent on input and involvement. When next you make a decision, at home or at work, use this criterion to suggest the most effective style.

Go To:
Beware: Change Imposed Is Change Opposed (1.9)
Decide the Best Method Before Making an Important Decision (3.11)
What Are the Characteristics of a Great Workplace? (4.6)

Action-Oriented Style

Working with many managers over the years, I have observed that those who are successful seem to share some notable characteristics. One of these is a belief and the practice that it is always better to do something than do nothing.

This action orientation is also not a bad principle for effective living. It works for two important reasons. First, when you take action, even though it may not be the best action, it puts you in control of the situation and forces others to respond to you rather than you responding to the situation. Second, when you take action, it changes the situation and creates opportunities that did not exist before you took the action.

Effective managers know intuitively that not all problems have an obvious solution and that if they make a first approximation action it will often change the situation markedly. It is then their responsibility to find the appropriate next action in the changed situation.

This action orientation and practice is clearly a key to success in the managerial role. Consider a popular management practice that is essentially passive, the open-door policy. I am rarely in an organization where managers do not have an explicitly stated open invitation for people to drop into the office. If you visit managers, they will often report that the people they would like to visit with them rarely come into their office. Instead, they seem to get a small stream of outspoken, tiresome people who have "issues." Many often report that these drop-ins not only waste their time but often break up their workflow and reduce their productivity.

Consider instead an active management practice that explicitly invites peoples' opinions, happens somewhat unpredictably and occurs in the employees' work area. Almost all people are more comfortable in their own workspace than in the manager's office. This tool is management by wandering around, a more informal version of another information gathering tool, the skip-level meeting.

Management by wandering around is a simple tool that requires high managerial interpersonal skill. If you are thinking of using this tool, consider the following elements to success. First, it is necessary to discuss with your direct reports that you are going to begin this practice and outline in some detail how you will use it. Failure to do so often results in confusion

Effective managers believe it is always better to do something rather than nothing.

by both managers and employees about just what it is you are doing and why. You might mention that you will tend to do it at a particular time, perhaps during the morning of one day and the afternoon of another, but there are no specific times. It is often useful to initiate such a brief conversation by making a positive, personal comment or by leading with a question that you believe will be of interest to the person.

The single most important skill to making this tool successful is the ability to be a good listener. You might practice using active listening with your significant other to prepare for "wandering." It is also important to listen but not make decisions, don't jump your chain of command and use your judgment about what and how to share information in response to questions people ask you. It is also fine to tell people that you don't know and to offer to find out and get back to them. If you make such a promise, make sure you fulfill it to keep the perception of a high say/do ratio.

Wandering is a rather sophisticated skill, and like any skill, practice and review will improve your performance. Here are some of the tactics that will improve the effectiveness of the tool. Over the course of time, it is important to make sure you are perceived to be visiting with a variety of people and not just a select few. Just visiting with some of your employees will quickly produce the perception of favoritism among the rest.

As your skill improves, you will notice that the simplicity and brevity of the questions you ask will markedly improve. Wandering is a tool to help you develop another effective management skill: directing people by asking shrewd questions. Many of the very best managers I have worked with avoid talking *at* people at all costs. They have learned that you can rarely change behavior by lecturing. Rather, they develop a repertory of questions designed to invite thoughtful input from people.

I once worked with the top manager at a 24/7 manufacturing facility. Over the first several months of his tenure, he developed a pattern of randomly dropping in and spending a couple hours wandering and visiting with people during off-shifts. He also suggested to the supervisors that they not trail him around. Using this tool, he was able to develop a shrewd understanding of employees' concerns. Careful to protect the source of the information, he often used it to initiate thoughtful discussion with his management team. Needless to say, he was highly regarded by employees and managers. He eventually phased out wandering because of the time it consumed and smoothly transitioned to skip-level meetings that produced much the same results.

Go To:
Improving Your Communications Through Active Listening (1.3)
SMART Action Plans Help Direct Work Toward Goals (3.8)
What Is Your Attitude Toward Work? (4.2)

2.7

Principles vs. Rules

"I don't do that — it's not in my job description" is an extremely unpleasant phrase to hear if you are a manager trying to accomplish something. It usually means "bad employee" to managers, but unfortunately the problem is more fundamental and partially of management's own creation.

We often hear that knowledge workers need to be managed with trust and not by force and yet we have inadvertently created systems that invite some workers, almost without exception the low performers, to use the aforementioned sentence. By focusing on rules and policies instead of principles, we have walked ourselves into the rules trap.

Policies and procedures are necessary for the efficient operation of organizations and are indispensable in some parts of the organization, but all too often such systems devolve into a huge set of almost unknowable rules. Consider the IRS tax code — It is at present unknowable by any one person. Consider the consequences and efforts to enforce these rules.

How does this type of thoughtless rule making happen? Policies, especially policies about people, are most often written in reaction to some unfortunate incident. Many times I have been in a meeting where some-one suggested that we need a policy to make sure something doesn't hap-pen again. This is a completely reactive style of management. Consider what message it conveys to people when we tell them what not to do instead of what to do.

There are two negative consequences of this reactionary rule writing. First, each rule is written without any consideration of what its unintend-ed consequences might be, particularly throughout the larger organiza-tion. Many times a rule that works perfectly in one part of the organiza-tion results in chaos in another part. This is a perfect example of solving a tactical problem and creating a strategic issue.

'Rules are for the obedience of fools and the guidance of wise men.'

- DOUGLAS BADER

Second, the manner in which such rules are written usually conveys the strong message to employees that management does not trust them and therefore they need detailed and specific instructions on how not to behave. In brief, they are dumb and cannot be expected to exercise com-mon sense. In my own experience, common sense is equally distributed throughout the population. One has only to pick up a newspaper and observe the egregious actions of people in positions of significant author-ity who appear to be functioning absent any common sense.

Consider how much more powerful principles are when used in the workplace. Principles invite people to find their own personal manner of enacting them. Look at the effects of a simple, positive rule such as "always say thank you" compared to a general principle such as "show respect for people." The first is narrow and inflexible and offers no oppor-tunity for consideration, thought or reflection. The latter allows each per-son to examine the basic tenet and adjust her behavior. Any system that elicits thoughtful consideration cannot be harmful.

From a more-strategic perspective, consider the following principles. They can be thought of as essential to the operation of an effective organ-ization:

1. The better informed people are, the better they perform.
2. The closer a decision is made to the work, the better the decision.

Rules can never be written cleverly enough that they cannot be subverted by creative people and thus rendered useless, particularly in providing guidance on ethical issues. How many times have you seen a difficult employee essentially gaming rules in a fashion that produces behavior that was the opposite of what was intended by the rule? My experience in the workplace is that this happens most frequently around issues of attendance and leave.

Rules can also produce a troubling sort of mindlessness when people act upon them in a rigid, thoughtless fashion. How many examples of poor customer service begin with a person saying, "I can't do that because our policy is..." Doing what is legal (rules) is not always ethical, but doing what is ethical (principles) is almost without exception legal.

A good example of the use of rules and principles is the issue of managing difficult employees. In this situation, we often begin such a process from the base of principles, but should we learn that the employee is resistant to change, we quickly switch to the rules-based approach of progressive discipline.

So managers must find a balance between the use of rules and the use of principles, keeping in mind that managing from principles is more difficult because it requires the thoughtful exercise of judgment and common sense. When making this decision, give thoughtful consideration to where we seek the absolute adherence to rules versus where we encourage the use of personal judgment driven by a guiding principle.

Go To:
One-on-One Feedback Is Vital for Your Employees (1.2)
Managing Troubled and Troublesome Employees (1.13)
Respectful Behavior (2.4)
Engagement and Decision Making (2.5)

2.8

Tactical to Strategic

There seem to be two reasons people become managers: Being very good at something (technical competence) and an ability to get things done (execution). These two characteristics are valued and rewarded in effective organizations. Unfortunately, if people advance far enough up the chain of command, these characteristics can cause problems.

As many consultants can attest, one major problem in organizations is the inability of many managers to think and act strategically. Executives often seem to be over involved in the mundane, detailed issues of getting the work done. I once worked with a CEO who headed an organization in dire condition and he was spending most of his time looking at spreadsheets. It was not a surprise that his former position was CFO. Comfort and security are found in these details, but when senior managers go to what is comfortable and safe, the absence of leadership at the top is quickly felt.

A major concern often voiced by employees is that they are being micro-managed. This is a good indication that their manager has not successfully learned how to delegate effectively and has failed to begin the transition to strategic thought.

Perhaps the greatest developmental challenge to becoming a manager is the understanding that part of your job is to work on the organization, not in the organization, to move from a tactical focus (getting the job done) to a strategic focus (making the organization perform better). The difference between a first-level manager and a CEO is the scope and proportion of time spent in the strategic function. An effective CEO will spend almost all of her time working on the organization. The process of working effectively on the organization is often called leadership.

Becoming a C-level manager, especially a CEO, is making another career change (the change from a technical position to the first managerial job was the previous career change). The job requires a high level of understanding of the context within which the organization functions, an ability to comprehend how every decision cascades throughout an organization with both positive and negative consequences, a keen perception of who the key stakeholders are and what each values and will fight to preserve.

The capacity for reflection is a key element of strategic thinking. However, reflection is not a characteristic that successful, hard-driving managers have been rewarded for, thus making the transition difficult for most managers. So, if you are intending to become a more strategic

---

Effective executives work on the organization, not in the organization.

---

thinker, reflect on these ideas.

Strategic thinkers read widely and are well informed. My best clients read the *Wall Street Journal* almost every day and a variety of general as well as industry-specific publications. They often suggest material to me that is valuable in my consulting practice. This exposure to a wide variety of viewpoints improves their larger understanding of the complex social, political and economic systems in which we function.

Strategic thinkers are also able "to walk in my moccasins before you judge me." They work to see issues from as many perspectives as possible and thus can develop strategies that are reality based and more likely to succeed. This ability also enhances their capacity to perceive and understand the inter-connectedness of the systems. This is the antithesis of the "single issue" viewpoint that shows no understanding of complexity and thus is more prey to the law of unintended consequences.

Strategic thinkers also operate from a well thought out and coherent set of principles that guide their behavior. We often refer to such principles as values. This is also a characteristic of all of the successful people I have encountered. Their values are the anchor that keeps their decision making consistent and ethical.

Yet another characteristic of strategic people is their ability to trust their intuition, the non-linear, emotional aspect of thought. They often "sense" the rightness or wrongness of an issue. I believe this is related to the ability to engage in inductive reasoning, thinking from many specific inputs to formulate a general overview of a situation. Often these intuitive and inductive aspects of an issue are very subtle and to be strategic means to cultivate these, listen to them and trust them. This seems to be a core characteristic of effective leaders.

Go To:
Candor Is a Valuable Trait in Successful Leaders (1.5)
How Managers Fail (2.11)
Leadership Is an Important Organizational Performance Driver (3.1)
Practicing Executive Wisdom (3.18)

2.9

Courage: Managers into Leaders

This series of segments began by reviewing how the industrial revolution gave rise to management and how the information economy has subsequently produced the knowledge worker. The currency of the knowledge worker is information and thus their tasks are almost exclusively mental rather than muscle.

The predominance of knowledge workers in the workplace has changed the nature of management. It is no longer possible to manage by force; managers must be skilled at managing by developing a workplace of trust. Knowledge workers have a much greater capacity to contribute good or ill to organizational performance. This is illustrated in the extreme measures companies now take to protect their systems when they discharge an employee and the speed with which Gen Xers depart companies they perceive are mistreating them.

Managing by trust at first appears a formidable challenge, but it is really quite natural in an information economy. Where change is happening rapidly, leaders must move to use principles rather than rules, to open communications and to engage people, particularly their front-line managers, in the decision-making process. The result of this trend is that management has become a principle-based art and that the idea of leadership throughout the organization has become more prevalent.

To some this may appear to be a too-soft form of management that precludes the ability of executives to make sweeping change without using a sometimes long and clumsy process. In actuality, managers, and particularly leaders, must have the ability and skills to recognize that a single operating style will not always be effective, and on occasion dramatic action will have to be taken without prior consultation.

The 4-H pledge gets it exactly right: head, heart, hands and health.

This brings us to the final and most important principle of management and the principle that largely defines leadership. Without this element all the others cannot be successfully enacted — courage.

In the absence of courage, management is simply a set of processes that will mindlessly continue and eventually render themselves out-of-date and obsolete to the detriment of the organization and its people. Reading studies of leadership, I am struck by how evidence of leadership is closely tied to recognizing that change is necessary, divining what that change should be and executing it in the face of serious and often reasonable resistance. This is not a strictly mental process; there is much here that is emotional and intuitive. So what are the elements that give some people courage when others are overcome by paralysis? Certainly, the principles we have discussed are often necessary, but what is the spark that makes it clear an action was courageous?

I am always impressed at how the 4-H pledge gets it exactly right: head, heart, hands and health. Human psychology consists of these four parts: 1. Head - our thoughts, cognitions; 2. Heart - our feelings, emotions; 3. Hands - our actions, behaviors; 4. Health - "a sound mind needs a sound body." The Roman poet's next line after "a sound mind..." is "Ask for a brave soul..."

Peter Drucker said that "managers do things right, leaders do the right thing." Courage is clearly the ability to "do the right thing." It is impossible to separate courage and leadership.

For courage to show itself, it is necessary that the person have a well-developed and realistic sense of self-worth. The lack of confidence inhibits action and overconfidence, which we often refer to as egotism, propels impulsive and thoughtless action without regard to the effects or consequences. People with self-confidence are often wise in their choice of mentors during their developmental years. This shows that their lives are journeys of self-discovery, always comparing their actions against the results and over time becoming more skilled at acting appropriately to each situation.

Fundamental to the development of self-worth is an explicit, well thought out set of ethical principles. Without such a moral compass, people have no coherent basis for directing their actions. Their behavior becomes completely situational and thus to some extent out of their control. These are people who are reacting to the immediacy of the moment without regard to its context or implications. Unfortunately, we have all worked with such people.

This then is a mixture of head and heart, using our minds to develop actions that elicit positive responses from the environment, thus reinforcing our perception of our personal worth.

This, however, does not get us to doing what is right. Often, the right decision comes wrapped in circumstances that have a very high emotional content. Recent work on leadership suggests that leaders are often formed out of emotionally powerful crucibles. These difficult circumstances present the opportunity to reflect upon who we believe we are and to rethink our understanding of ourselves. My own experience with leaders suggests that all such persons have one or more of these events occur at critical times in their lives and are willing to discuss these and reflect on how they altered the course of their lives. These powerful emotional events provide leaders with an understanding of their values and motivations and give them the heart to know intuitively what is right.

The essential ingredients are to have the confidence, the ethical foundation and the heart to know and feel what is right. But we infer courage from actions, not thoughts or feelings. Understanding how to deploy one's self is the final key element of leadership.

What defines the person who has the head and heart is the hands, the ability to convert thought and emotion into purposeful action. Such people are golden in organizations in these turbulent organizational times.

Go To:
Respectful Behavior (2.4)
Values of the Ethical Manager (2.12)
Never Waste a Good Crisis (3.19)

Why Ethical Behavior Is Profitable

I first wrote this segment about 20 years ago, and have revised it several times since. In each revision I have had to replace the names of earlier companies that have behaved egregiously unethically with more recent companies. How distressing it is that this litany of failed business ethics goes on and on.

Nearly every national survey conducted on the topic of professional trust shows that large numbers of Americans believe business executives are dishonest. For more than two decades I have been working closely with businesses, public sector organizations and nonprofits, and my own experience is not consistent with this perception. I have found business people to be thoughtful, caring individuals who are often as concerned about ethics and customers as profits. Is this a regional phenomenon? I think not. What is clear is that businesses, like people, must formulate and live by a clear set of ethics if they intend to survive and thrive.

A reasonable assumption for a person or business is that ethical behavior is profitable, a belief held by many people. I think there is ample evidence to support this belief. Let me elaborate on three ways that ethical behavior is profitable.

Ethical behavior is personally profitable. The literature in the psychology of human behavior is replete with evidence that self-esteem is an essential ingredient of effective functioning. The argument goes something like this. There is one person in the world that you must like, one person that you must respect and one person you must hold in high regard: the person you see in the mirror each morning.

There are examples in our society of people, some very young, who hold themselves in such disregard that they end their own lives. Conversely, it is clear to most of us that people who function well in the world of work have a measure of self-confidence that contributes to their success. What is the foundation of this self-esteem? Integrity.

We build self-respect through our own ethical behavior. The Bard said it best: "To thy own self be true, and thus it follows as the night the day, thou can'st not then be false to any man." A better piece of advice does not exist. I think most of us know that people who are not honest with themselves, who deceive themselves, begin to lose track of who they are.

When that happens people are in serious trouble. It is important for us to feel good about and to respect ourselves. Doing what is right is the foundation for that self-esteem.

It can also be argued that **ethical behavior is interpersonally profitable**. We live in a world of people. Take away the people and what is left? Most of what we do in our lives is for people we respect or love. People are the most important element in our world. How do we build firm and lasting relationships with people — through ethical behavior.

Businesses must formulate and live by a clear set of ethics if they intend to survive and thrive.

Think of those you respect and trust. Who are they? The people who behave with integrity toward you. One simple definition of integrity is doing what you say you will do when you say you will do it. These are the people in our environment that we hold in high regard.

I refer to this definition of integrity as the say/do ratio. Each of us knows persons with a high say/do ratio and we know that they deliver. Their word is their bond. Consider the axiom what you give is what you get. To a large extent, we create the world around us by how we treat our friends, colleagues and loved ones. The say/do ratio is one of the best examples of this principle in action. Mark Twain said it well: "Do what is right. It will gratify some people and astonish the rest."

Finally, **ethical behavior is organizationally profitable**. Every day each of us touches and is touched upon by many organizations. Examine those that you hold in high regard and compare them with those that you have negative feelings toward. We are all experts on one thing, how we are treated.

Many businesses appear not to have learned this lesson. Every thoughtful person has a mental list of businesses that they will not trade with as well as a list that they prefer to use. What determines the list? How we are treated as customers, clients, patients or consumers. For many years, marketing research has shown that when a business treats a customer badly, that customer will tell many people about the incident. No wonder so many businesses fail.

Another lesson that many in the world of work have never learned is that how you treat your employees is how they treat the customers (employees call this the "plumber's rule"). As an organizational consultant, I have found that a good measure of the climate of a company is how they treat me at first contact. Some organizations are courteous and helpful, while others make it very clear that you are an unwelcome bother. In their book about productivity in American companies, *In Search of Excellence*, Tom Peters and Robert Waterman wrote, "Treat people as adults. Treat them as partners; treat them with respect. Treat them — not capital spending and automation — as the primary source of productivity gains."

I think these examples make a strong case for the practice of ethical behavior. First, because doing what is right builds self-confidence and allows us to sleep with ourselves at night. Second, because respect and trust between people are a product of ethical behavior. Someone once said that a person is only as good as his ability to make his word valuable through his behavior. Finally, because organizations touch on two types of people: employees and customers. Employees will only give us their best when we treat them ethically and customers will take their business elsewhere if we are not ethical.

Go To:
The Basics of an Effective Management Style (1.1)
Leadership Is an Important Organizational Performance Driver (3.1)
Improving Your Personal and Professional Productivity (5.1)
Take the Time to Stop and Reflect on Success (5.6)

2.11

How Managers Fail

Considerable evidence from practice and research shows that three factors predict the long-term success of managers (in this context we are using managers to describe anyone who has managerial responsibility from front-line supervisors to executives). These three factors are: Technical competence, interpersonal skills and ethical behavior.

Interestingly enough, ethical behavior and interpersonal skills are much better predictors of success than technical competence. The observation that most people are promoted to managerial positions exclusively on their technical competence explains the wide range of managerial performance in most organizations. When the reasons for managerial failure are reviewed, however, ethical issues explain much of the failure.

In general, managers fail for four major reasons: misuse of power, inappropriate emotional behavior, the escalation of commitment and the diffusion of authority.

Managing people in any organization is an exercise in the wise use of power. Managers have considerable power over their employees. Not only do managers have the power to deprive employees of the job itself, but they have immense influence over their peoples' day-to-day work lives. They can help people succeed or make them fail, and they are the largest source of stress in the workplace. Collectively, the behavior of managers is the largest contributor to what we call morale and drives how people think, feel and act on the job.

The issue of power is closely related to the degree to which managers are willing to trust their employees. This is inversely related to the degree of formal control that is exerted within the organization. Recently, I was in an organization where several senior managers were reviewing a six-page dress code that the senior executive group decided was necessary because of some dress infractions. Aside from working very hard to produce a set of rules that people were sure to find insulting, it was clear that this particular senior executive group was not focused on the important strategic issues that were confronting the company. This is a classic example of executives doing the wrong things. It's also a good example of managers writing rules to solve specific problems rather than confronting the small number of people who are violating the informal understandings about the workplace.

Stress makes people stupid. We know from many years of studies that levels of stress that are either too low (boredom) or too high have very negative effects on performance. In the contemporary workplace, we see very few examples of low levels of stress, but more than enough of excessive stress. Much of this stress is imposed by managers who are emotional bullies. I have interviewed hundreds of employees in the past two decades, and too many of them have stories about being bullied in the workplace. The most striking aspect of these stories is that the emotional content remains even if the incident took place many years ago. Please remember, "When the temperature rises, the light dims." Decisions and communications that take place in the heat of emotion are usually very poor and likely to have quite negative effects on people.

Ethical behavior and interpersonal skills are better predictors of success than technical competence.

Over time, I have collected a list of employees' most disliked behaviors in managers. These are sarcasm, not listening and/or ignoring, sniping, punishing "all for one," breaking confidence, asking for input when the decision has been made, asking for input on trivial decisions, not explaining why, writing a policy to solve a problem and coming to meetings late. All of these behaviors are about misuse of power or emotional manipulation.

The escalation of commitment is an unethical behavior that is seen most often in executives. This occurs when a manager makes a bad decision and rather than acknowledging the mistake and reversing or correcting it, keeps pouring more resources into trying to make it work. Many case studies of this behavior are used in business schools and often the outcome of this over-investment of ego in a failing idea is catastrophic for the organization.

The fourth reason for managerial failure is diffusion of responsibility. The 19th century political philosopher, Edmund Burke, stated, "All that is necessary for evil to prevail is for good men to do nothing." Many managers fail because they will not accept responsibility for corporate decisions and divert blame onto senior management. These managers do not believe that they have an obligation to support corporate decisions and will undermine and ridicule decisions with which they personally disagree. Widely practiced, such behavior builds enormous mistrust in employees and leads to chaos. The failure of people to accept responsibility can lead to the most horrific consequences. Perhaps the most terrible example in the 20th century is the Holocaust.

Go To:
The Basics of an Effective Management Style (1.1)
Respectful Behavior (2.4); Defining Executive Wisdom (3.17)
A Multi-Dimensional View of Motivation and Morale (4.1)

2.12

Values of the Ethical Manager

Managers have two major tools to influence the behavior of people in the workplace: communication and decision making. These tools can be used in an ethical or unethical manner. Consider these essential ingredients necessary to high performance in the managerial role.

Aretha Franklin had a wonderful hit in the rock era: "Respect," in which she sang, "Tell me what it means to me." Excellent managers are always respectful of the people they work for and with. I have occasionally heard people state "you have to earn my respect." This philosophy is patent nonsense and flies in the face of all research about human interaction. Research on human interaction shows that human behavior is highly reciprocal. In short, what you give is what you get. Respect begets respect and disrespect begets disrespect. You can change the behavior of a disrespectful colleague by treating them respectfully (this will work only if you have patience). Lists of most-disliked behaviors by employees are mostly lists of disrespectful behaviors.

What basic beliefs must we hold in order to operate on the above principle of reciprocity? First and foremost, we must believe that almost all people are trustworthy and thus deserving of our trust from the beginning of our relationship. Second, we must believe that in almost every situation it is better for people to be informed than to remain in ignorance. Third, we must believe it is better for us to do things with others rather than to them. These are key elements in the construction of trust. They are also key ingredients in the repertory of high-performance managers.

The key to managing is developing and maintaining effective working relationships. This is not an easy task. New managers usually struggle to find an appropriate middle ground between being too distant and controlling or too close and familiar. Managers who are too friendly with their employees are often well liked but not respected, whereas managers that are too distant are not liked or respected.

Both of these styles are ineffective in getting people to do things for you, and the best definition of management is "getting people to do things for you." Over-controlling, authoritarian and loose, laissez-faire managers produce types of failure that are distinctly different. The over-controlling manager is often perceived to be one who does not respect the opinions of others and drives heavy levels of stress in her employees. The laissez-faire manager by contrast creates a work environment where expectations are so ambiguous that people are very frustrated. In interviews, many people actually report that they prefer the authoritarian manager because, although stress levels are high, work is getting done.

Another issue for the new manager is to fully understand that the position carries with it a higher level of responsibility to the organization. It is imperative that the manager act in the best interests of the organization. Not to do so is a major type of unethical behavior. The people we read about in the newspapers who have destroyed companies and the lives of their employees have not acted in the best interests of those organizations. Likewise, the manager who basically says to his employees, "I'm not responsible, senior management made me do it," is acting in a wholly irresponsible and unethical manner.

Consider these six ethical principles:

1. Obey the law
2. Tell the truth
3. Show respect for people
4. First, do no harm
5. Practice participation — not paternalism
6. Always act when you have the responsibility to do so

Obey the law. This seems a simple principle until we examine it. The basic question posed is, what is the law? The law as we know it is so large and complex as to be almost unknowable, even for attorneys, and it is always changing, albeit slowly. Working in organizations, I am sometimes confronted with situations where two competent, well-informed attorneys are giving opposite advice on an issue.

Such a situation also raises the issue of the difference between legal and ethical. Legal and ethical are not identical; what is ethical is usually legal, but what is legal is not always ethical. We read in the papers every day of instances where people or organizations are doing things that are legal but ethically questionable. Large governmental bureaucracies seem to be particularly vulnerable to this type of behavior because of the diffusion of responsibility.

This diffusion in large organizations often leads to a practice that I call "rule-bound behavior." Rule-bound behavior is when people mindlessly follow rules that are patently absurd. "Any fool can make a rule and every fool will follow it." How to solve this conundrum? The best advice is to try to be consistent and reasonable because, in general, the law is consistent and reasonable.

Tell the truth. This is another simple idea that grows rather complex on examination. "Do not tell untruths" is a good solid rule that works most of the time. We have all seen instances of untruths coming home to roost. Unfortunately, there are two types of untruths: commission and omission. Our previous rule only works for untruths of commission, not omission. Each of us has a censor in his or her head that systematically edits what we say. We know that telling everyone exactly what we think or feel all the time is naive and insensitive. However, what we withhold is often very important. To remain silent in some situations, to not speak or act, may be unethical. Be sure you are aware of your censor and know why and how it is working.

An interesting test of an organization's culture is the answer to the question, "What is secret and why?" There should be a reasonable middle ground. Some things need to be kept confidential whereas others do not. Defining these categories is not an easy task, but the process of deciding what is secret or not is a healthy one for organizations. The way to keep organizations honest is to keep them open. Is anyone surprised that secretive government organizations are often in the news for their ethical misconduct? Secrecy creates the opportunity for abuse.

Show respect for people — practice the Golden Rule. If our behavior is mutually reciprocal, then the more we can treat others with respect, the better our lives will become. From time to time, there are articles in the print media about either the decline or resurgence of courtesy in America.

I often tell businesspeople that everyone — customer, client or patient — is an expert in evaluating how he is treated. There is hardly a better piece of advice than, "Treat others as you would like to be treated."

Managers have two major tools to influence the behavior of people in the workplace: communication and decision making. These tools can be used in an ethical or unethical manner.

First, do no harm is the first precept of medical ethics: In Latin, *Primum non nocere*. Another simple precept to understand but difficult to practice because sometimes we must harm people. For example, terminating a non-performing employee may be harmful to that person. It is important that we weigh the costs and benefits of such actions before we act. In this case, a greater harm to fellow employees and the company may result if we do not terminate. The Star Trek character Spock said it well, "The good of the many versus the good of the one."

Practice engagement — not paternalism. The essence of modern management is to involve people in the process of work: To do things with people, not to them. Mushroom management is an example of paternalism. "I must be a mushroom; people keep me in the dark and feed me BS." Inviting people to provide input into decision making improves the quality of the information base and gives people a sense of ownership of the decision and still preserves the prerogative of the manager to make the decision. Yet another effect of involvement is that it reduces stress. We are most stressed when we feel out of control. Giving people some element of control over their work lives reduces work-related stress appreciably.

Always act when you have the responsibility to do so. A central tenet of good management is that it is better to act, to take the initiative, than to react. Some of the most serious ethical abuses take place when good people do nothing. The responsibility to act is a necessary condition to the maintenance of a free society as well as an ethical organization. Allowing ethical abuses to go unchallenged is one of the most dangerous shortcomings people in an organization can practice. Small abuses, gone unreported, tend to encourage larger and larger abuses until a situation has deteriorated beyond control.

These six principles are a set of values. Such a set of values is often difficult to put into practice as a manager. How can we create conditions in a work environment that facilitate the practice of these values?

In the last few years the term "stakeholder" has begun to be used in business literature. The definition of a stakeholder is wonderfully telegraphic. A stakeholder is one who has a stake in an issue, decision or organization. James O'Toole, a business management professor at the University of Southern California, has introduced the idea of "stakeholder symmetry." Such an ethical practice begins with the definition of the various stakeholders in an issue that might have ethical implications, then proceeding to examine the stakes they hold and the positive and negative effects of the action on these stakeholders. Such an analysis does not necessarily lead to a solution, but it does cause us to examine in a thoughtful way the implications of our acts.

Go To:
Principles vs. Rules (2.7)
Leadership Is an Important Organizational Performance Driver (3.1)
Take the Time to Stop and Reflect on Success (5.6)

What Predicts Managerial Success

For some years, I have been working with a variety of companies to assist them in the development of managers. I have worked closely with managers who are having problems functioning, helped build the skills of managers who are interested in improving their functioning and assisted companies in the identification of people who have high potential as managers.

I have also had the opportunity to see how managers grow and develop across time. This experience has caused me to form some rather clear impressions of what predicts managerial success, as well as some ideas about how managers fail and what the skills of successful managers seem to be. These experiences are consistent with the findings of longitudinal research on managerial success and failure.

The prediction of managerial success is an issue of great importance in today's turbulent workplace. More than ever before, managers are being required to perform in ways that reduce turnover and absenteeism, increase productivity, increase employee engagement, introduce and use new technology effectively and manage a more-diverse and skilled workforce. All this when the absolute number of managers in most workplaces is declining. In short, fewer managers are doing more complex and demanding tasks. The identification and development of talented managers is critical to the short and particularly the long-term success of companies in competitive business environments.

Even as this is the case, each of us knows from experience that the quality of managers in any company varies widely. In most companies I have worked with there are usually a few truly excellent managers. These are the people that it is a delight to work for and with. They make coming to work in the morning a pleasure. They are people builders, and those of us who have had the opportunity to work with such managers have benefited in our levels of competence, job satisfaction and self-esteem. Conversely, most of us have had the unfortunate experience of working with managers who produce exactly the opposite effects in employees. "What mood is s/he in today?" is the best description of the worst of them. They are un-caring, cause stress that we carry home and often drive us to behave in ways that violate our sense of what is right and wrong.

How can the reasonable people who run companies continue to make so many mistakes in the promotion of managers? How tragic this is, especially because we know that employee morale and productivity is largely driven by how our immediate supervisor treats us.

The reason for such a wide variability in the quality of managers is that companies promote on a single criterion: competence. Most people are moved to managerial roles because of their competence in their chosen role. Then they are most often left to succeed or fail without much help from anyone. Thus, the best engineer becomes the manufacturing manager, the best salesperson the director of marketing, the best secretary the office administrator, the best nurse the nurse-manager and on and on. Yet research shows that promoting on competence alone produces mixed results in the quality of managers. What then are appropriate criteria or predictors of managerial performance?

Longitudinal research tracking the careers of managers over decades carried out by the Center for Creative Leadership and at AT&T shows that the best predictors of success in management are: competence, integrity and people skill.

Competence, the usual criterion for promoting managers, seems self-evident. It is difficult to manage someone when you don't understand the job they are performing. In general, this also applies to executive leadership. Research and history show that the very best leaders have a deep understanding of the core business and most likely have spent most of their careers in the organization they are leading.

The second predictor of managerial success is **integrity**. The simplest definition of integrity is the best one: I will do what I say I will do when I say I will do it. If I cannot I will tell you as soon as possible. I refer to this measure of integrity as the say/do ratio. If you think for a moment about the people you work with that you respect and trust, they have a very good say/do ratio. You can depend on them to do it and if they cannot, they let you know as soon as possible. This is not just a measure of integrity, but it is also a measure of how well people can manage their own behavior. People who have a high say/do ratio have strategies to make sure that phone calls are returned, letters and reports are sent as promised, they arrive on time for meetings, etc. In short, work gets done as promised. This behavior multiplied by many people is the heart of follow through and walking the talk.

This is an important measure because it also tells us about peoples' understanding of the relationship between their behavior and its effects. Many people do not have a high say/do ratio because they don't perceive the effects on other people of not doing so. They do not see the disruption that not delivering on promises causes customers, co-workers and employees. Also, these are people who usually have difficulty ever acknowledging a mistake. People with a high say/do ratio realize that sometimes events interfere with getting things done as promised and they acknowledge these lapses. They are capable of saying, "I made a mistake" or "I was wrong." How infuriating it is to work with someone who is never wrong, who never makes a mistake.

Another important aspect of the say/do ratio is the so-called plumber's rule. People do what their boss does. A manager is a powerful role model. If you want your people to be at work on time, you had better be at work on time. There are not two sets of rules, one for the managers and another for the workers. People watch and emulate the behavior of their managers and managers set the standard of what is acceptable through their behavior. Surely people who cannot do what they expect others to do have no business trying to manage others.

The say/do ratio is not an exhaustive definition of integrity. Ethical behavior is central to personal, professional and managerial success. It is important to understand that people who have a high quality of life almost always have a well-formulated set of values they use to self-manage.

The third predictor of managerial success is **people skill**. If management is "getting people to do things for you," then it requires a well-developed set of "working with people" skills. In recent years, two separate but related perspectives defining what people skill in management is have emerged.

The managerial approach defines people skill on the base of the two most critical managerial skills: the ability to communicate effectively and to make decisions. The general principles that drive this approach are twofold: 1. The better informed people are, the better they perform, and 2. The closer a decision is made to the work, the better the decision. Communication is the tool we use to manage information and decision making is the tool for sharing responsibility downward in the organization.

The second approach to people skill is the rapidly emerging research and practice on emotional intelligence or EQ. EQ is defined as the capacity to: 1. Recognize one's own and other's feelings, 2. Manage emotions in ourselves and others and 3. Generate motivation in the workplace to help others become more productive, effective and self-fulfilled. The core element of EQ is relationship management, which encompasses inspirational leadership, influence, developing others, acting as a change catalyst, managing conflict, building bonds and encouraging teamwork and collaboration.

The power of these two complementary approaches is they are skill based. People can learn to be better communicators and decision makers and can learn to improve their EQs. In the first approach, the basic principles of communication are based on what people in the workplace need to know and when and how they can be involved in the decision-making process. In the case of EQ, it is possible using 360-degree assessments to provide people with accurate information to enhance their ability to change.

Thus, the three predictors of managerial success across time are: competence, integrity and people skill. It is also clear from the research that the major reasons for managerial failure are either violations of integrity/ethics or an inability to work effectively with others.

Go To:
Courage: Managers into Leaders (2.9)
Values of the Ethical Manager (2.12)
What Is Your Attitude Toward Work? (4.2)
If You See a Bathroom, Use It! (5.2)

Unit 3:
Leadership and Executive Behavior

Leadership is highly valued in our society and the literature on this topic is extensive. The first five segments in this unit present an introduction to the import of leadership and several different models of leadership. Segment 3.5 presents a reflective model based on recent thought and is a compelling set of developmental steps to becoming a leader.

1. Leadership Is an Important Organizational Performance Driver
2. Principle-Centered Leadership Has Benefits
3. A Personal Model of Leadership
4. Leadership as an Organizational Process
5. Leadership: A Journey of Self-Awareness

Much has been written on the difference between leadership and management. Clearly, people who do not hold positions of authority in organizations can exert leadership. We are all familiar with the positive and negative effects of informal leaders in organizations. In an organization, the greatest opportunity for leadership exists for those in positions at the top. One has only to open the newspaper to realize there is a great need to improve the quality of leadership throughout our organizations.

The second set consisting of eight segments presents and discusses what is perhaps Peter Drucker's last and best article on the core practices of effective executives. In these, I have tried to expand and add more detail to the basic ideas so that potential leaders can understand how to effectively enact this important role.

6. In Praise of Peter Drucker
7. Best For the Company or You — Is It the Same?
8. SMART Action Plans Help Direct Work Toward Goals
9. Good Leaders Take Responsibility For Communication
10. It's Important to Give Employees Vital Information
11. Decide the Best Method Before Making an Important Decision
12. Focus on Opportunities and Run Good Meetings
13. Effective Executives Think and Say "We," Not "I," In the Workplace

For those of you interested in reflecting more deeply on leadership, the third set of five segments explore the nature of executive wisdom. These are more philosophical and are designed to nurture reflection. The segment on the information continuum will help clarify the distinction among data, information, knowledge and wisdom.

14. Executive Wisdom: Context
15. The Information Continuum
16. Executive Wisdom Involves Balancing Knowledge
17. Defining Executive Wisdom
18. Practicing Executive Wisdom

The last group is a collection of miscellaneous material that is more related to the practice of leadership. The first is closely related to Drucker's advice to put your best people on your greatest opportunities: Never waste a good crisis. The second is an overview of a type of mentoring that is appropriate for an executive and organization that is committed to a management development and succession process. Third is an overview of the three sectors that constitute the modern economy: private-for-profit, private-nonprofit and public. A look at the use of consulting in business and an analysis of the perils of being a "nice" manager round out the unit.

19. Never Waste a Good Crisis
20. Harness the Power of Mentoring in Your Business
21. Organizations Come in Three Varieties
22. Understanding and Using Consulting as a Competitive Advantage
23. How 'Nice' Managers Unknowingly Cause Havoc

Leadership Is an Important Organizational Performance Driver

Having worked with more than 300 companies over two decades, one begins to understand that there are some fundamental principles about organizations that do not seem to be written in texts or articles.

People who study cognition refer to this type of information as experiential or tacit knowledge; sailors call it "local knowledge." It is clear that people with a large fund of tacit knowledge perform better in organizations because of this deeper understanding. Virtually all of this type of information about organizations is learned "on the job" of becoming an executive. Such principles as, "it's usually better if an employee has one boss," "the flatter an organizational structure the easier to communicate vertically," "organizations change only from the top down" and "if the business model is simple and widely understood, people and the organization will perform better," are often unspoken but understood at an intuitive level by high-performing persons.

Perhaps the premier of these chunks of tacit wisdom is "the most powerful variable driving organizational performance is leadership." I once heard an internationally respected consultant note that the best and quickest manner to assess the performance of a company is to spend an intense half day with the CEO. Needless to say, the person running such an interview must be highly skilled and have a huge fund of tacit organizational knowledge to obtain this result.

It is widely understood that an organization is only as good, or as bad, as its leader. When we read about deeply troubled organizations, one need only look to the values and behavior of the leader. Great organizations are led by executives that behave consistently from a set of pristine values.

Successfully running an organization of any size and type is an exercise in the wise use of power. The wise use of power is perhaps the best definition of leadership. Studying a person's ability to deploy this power is the study of leadership.

Americans in general are uncomfortable with the idea and exercise of power. This is largely because of our history and belief in equality and individual opportunity. Becoming an effective leader means beginning to understand the nature of power in organizations and how to use it in the best interests of the stakeholders.

Thoughtful people moving into executive positions often struggle with this issue. To them they are still the same person they were the day before the promotion. However, to many people in the organization they have now assumed a role that carries with it some mythic significance. The most immediate and troubling manifestation of this phenomenon is that many people start telling them what they want to hear, not what they need to hear. Close and trusted colleagues begin to "spin" their communications with the leader. This is even more the case when the leader is also the owner. One of the reasons executives engage consultants is that they need someone to confide in who will speak the truth with them.

It is widely understood that an organization is only as good, or as bad, as its leader.

Helping executives to fully comprehend and deploy this invisible but powerful tool is a significant challenge for a consultant. I have worked closely with many people moving into organizational leadership positions and almost all underestimate the power of their new position. Those who come to understand the power of the position and learn how to deploy it wisely become leaders. Those who deny the existence of this power are the greatest abusers of their power. Carry out a personal experiment. Ask yourself, "Which executives in my organization comprehend and deploy their power wisely?" Applying this new mental model can lead you to some striking insights about leadership.

What are the effects of leadership? Warren Bennis, who has written widely and deeply about leadership, notes that organizational leadership has four profound effects. Leaders create an environment where:
- People feel significant
- Learning and competence matter
- People are part of a community
- Work-life is exciting

I find it interesting that two of the four criteria are about how people feel. Food for thought.

Keeping these in mind and using this set of criteria for leadership is a worthwhile exercise as we embark on this multi-column journey of discovery about leadership.

Go To:
Courage: Managers into Leaders (2.9)
Why Ethical Behavior Is Profitable (2.10)
What Are the Characteristics of a Great Workplace? (4.6)

Principle-Centered Leadership Has Benefits

In the previous segment, we began to explore the nature of leadership, focusing on the wise use of power in organizations. Many thoughtful people have written cogently about leadership. If you read in this area, you probably have your favorite. In this piece, we will examine trait models and principle-centered models of leadership.

I once saw a bumper sticker that elicited a major belly laugh: "God, please let me be as good a person as my dog thinks I am." This is a perfect description of trait models of leadership. These models are derived by asking people, "What are the personal characteristics of leaders?" I have carried out this exercise many times in executive development settings and the results are always strikingly similar.

The most frequently used descriptors are: Integrity, courage, vision, openness, fairness, determination, focus, motivational, lead by example, communicator, consensus builder, caring, self-controlled, smart, imaginative, competent, mature, independent, risk taker, etc. The process produces lists of characteristics that can most aptly be described as "walking on water." This is a useful exercise because it demonstrates vividly that no one can possibly meet such a set of criteria. It is a flawed model of leadership because it offers no concrete suggestions about what to do to be a leader other than to be a perfect person (as your dog believes).

Inductive analyses bring us to a small set of principles that leaders seem to use as the basis for their behavior.

However, a careful, inductive analysis of these characteristics can bring us to a small set of principles that leaders seem to use as the basis for their behavior. Much has been written about this "principle-centered" leadership.

The above list can be grouped into three distinct themes: Personal competence, communication/people skills and integrity. Interestingly, the list is very similar to the three characteristics of a professional that I described in "Improving your personal and professional productivity" (5.1). However, the elements are more global and strategic in their basic nature.

Personal competence refers to the fact that leaders are perceived to have both concrete and tacit knowledge of the industry, the organization and the people that compose that organization. They are capable of seeing the broad and interrelated scope of all three of these aspects. As a consultant, I am constantly impressed at how difficult it is for people to imagine walking in another's shoes and also to assume a truly global perspective. In general, people are most comfortable in the details and analyzing the world only from their bias.

The inability to recognize one's own bias or to adopt a strategic perspective are major barriers to the development of leaders. Quoting Isaac Newton and speaking of the discovery of the physics of relativity, Albert Einstein is reputed to have said, "I could see so far because I stood on the shoulders of giants." Stakeholders trust the leaders of their organization will have this capacity to profit from and integrate the ideas and work of others into their performance as leaders. I believe one key behavior of leaders is that they all seem to be avid readers who read both widely and deeply.

In organizational audits, the most frequently occurring concern is usually the poor quality of communication within the company. Leaders tacitly understand that everything they do and say is a powerful form of communication and in acknowledging this, they are very thoughtful in the deployment of their time. When people move into leadership positions, they still believe that they are the same person. However, this is not the case; because of the perceived power of their position, everything they say and do is keenly observed and discussed by employees. Employees use this information to evaluate the person, the organization and the direction of the organization, and often refer to this as "walking the talk." This is perhaps the most powerful form of communication that an executive has in her/his repertory. For some it seems to be the hardest to use effectively, for only through their behavior can leaders "set the bar high."

People want to be proud, not ashamed, of the organizations for which they work. I recently spoke with a person in an organization where an employee tore up a 40-year award in front of his co-workers and stated that for the first time in all those decades he was not proud to work there. Leaders must manage the integrity of the organization. In all organizations, we see the operation of the "plumber's rule." If the leaders are people of integrity, the whole organization follows that model. This means that the leader's decisions must be ethically transparent to the whole organization. A visible example in too many organizations today is that the level of compensation of senior executives can no longer be justified to the rank and file. Leading an organization is about building trust, and the types of trust-busting behaviors are too numerous to list. For an in-depth analysis of ethical management, please review the three-part series in Unit 2.

A developing trend in management is to move away from rule-based systems to principle-based systems. This approach is an answer to the entitlement disease that some organizations are experiencing because it refocuses people on their responsibilities instead of their rights. The greatest strength of this approach is that it invites people to be the best they can be. For this type of management philosophy to work, it must be powerfully modeled by the leaders.

Go To:
Courage: Managers into Leaders (2.9)
Why Ethical Behavior Is Profitable (2.10)
What Are the Characteristics of a Great Workplace? (4.6)

A Personal Model of Leadership

One of the most lucid writers on leadership over the past 30 years is Warren Bennis. The strength of his perspective on leadership is that he casts it into a very personal mold, a mold that makes sense to the individual, a mold that we can get our hearts and minds around and translate into day-to-day behavior.

After studying a sample of leaders, he concluded that leaders manage four things: attention, meaning, trust and self. The elegant simplicity and economy of his model is its greatest strength. People can learn to do this.

Bennis states that the first leadership competence is the management of attention through a set of intentions or a vision in the sense of outcome, goal or direction. For example, I once worked with the owner/CEO of a small company who had several individually capable senior managers, but they functioned poorly as a management team. He could never get them working together on the same page at the same time. They often seemed to work at cross-purposes. Watching his management meetings, the reason became clear. At each meeting, he would present his seventeen No. 1 priorities for the company. Each manager was then choosing the two to three priorities he or she thought most important and all were naturally making different choices based on the needs of their portion of the organization. What a great way to make a group of capable people look like a bunch of uncoordinated fools. He was not managing their attention by presenting a simple, clear message about what was of over-arching importance to him.

The area of employee motivation is nebulous. Everyone seems to have an idea about what motivates employees. Most of these ideas are based on each person's experience and perspective. Many of these beliefs are wrong or naïve. However, a growing literature suggests that at some level people are basically existential: They want to find meaning in their lives; they want to be proud of where they work.

Leaders understand they must manage meaning to align people within the organization. A skilled leader I helped with a turn-around, after some thoughtful assessment of the company's needs, adopted a simple but powerful message that became his mantra: focus and fix. Everyone who interacted with him understood that the conversation or meeting would end with that statement, and he or she was expected to have a clear, coherent response. In this manner, he made people understand that the company was in distress and that each of their actions contributed to either the solution or the problem. This brought focus, urgency and discipline to the company.

After studying a sample of leaders, Bennis concluded that leaders manage four things: attention, meaning, trust and self.

In a knowledge-driven economy, we manage through trust, not force. Trust is essential to running a high-performance organization. The management of trust is the third aspect of leadership. The main driver of trust is what I call the say/do ratio. People would much rather follow individuals who are consistent and predictable in their behavior, even if they disagree with them, than someone who is unpredictable. The say/do ratio — "do what you say you are going to do when you say you are going to do it" — is a reliable and accurate measure of consistency as well as a powerful communication tool. In your own workspace, ask yourself, "Who do I trust and mistrust the most?" The say/do ratio defines the difference. Many, including myself, consider the say/do ratio a simple and fundamental measure of personal integrity. It can also be a powerful competitive advantage for an organization that is seeking to build close relationships with customers, clients or patients.

Reflecting on these first three aspects of leadership one is struck at how interrelated they seem to be; the core components and examples are highly congruent. Mr. Bennis wisely integrates this perception in his fourth aspect of leadership: The management of self. The most important personal question for leaders is: What message are you sending throughout the organization by what you are doing? In the previous example, the executive was making unmistakably clear that the organization was troubled and that everyone needed to step up and proactively engage in the change effort.

In developing leadership, the management of self is the starting place. There are 168 hours in a week. How are you spending them? How are you deploying your most precious commodity, your time? Are you communicating direction by managing attention? Are you defining building motivation by defining meaning? Are you developing trust through superb communications? In brief, are you managing yourself?

Go To:
Respectful Behavior (2.4)
If You See a Bathroom, Use It! (5.2)
Self-Talk to Success or Failure? (5.4)

3.4

Leadership as an Organizational Process

Some time ago, Jim Collins' book *Good to Great* was on the business bestseller list for more than two years. For my clients who are readers, I strongly recommend it.

Mr. Collins defines five levels of leadership in organizations. What he has done is find several examples of leaders who have driven huge, long-term improvements in the operating performance of Fortune 500 companies. These are difficult to find, in stark contrast to the daily reports of executives who have utterly destroyed companies and organizations.

Mr. Collins' findings suggest that an examination of leadership as an organizational development endeavor is appropriate, particularly because his study shows *what* high performance executives have done but has failed to clearly delineate *how* they have done it.

Leaders work within some organizational context, be it a company, a unit of government or a nonprofit organization. The purpose of their leadership might be modest, such as the better performance of a small business or grand such as the reformation of an economy. In each case, they are engaged in the management of some type of goal-driven change process. Thus, it is valuable to reflect on the process skills and knowledge a leader must bring to the table to drive positive change. The model I am suggesting has five essential ingredients.

The first ingredient is a keen understanding of the zeitgeist. Zeitgeist is a lovely German term that denotes the "spirit of the times." It is very clear that leaders have an acute understanding of the geo-political, industrial, organizational and cultural contexts within which they are operating. Isaac Newton is reputed to have said, referring to the paradigm shift he created, "I could see so far because I stood on the shoulders of giants." Leaders have a great breadth of knowledge that often rises to the level of wisdom. Virtually all the people I have worked with who I consider leaders are voracious readers and their reading pattern is at once both wide and deep.

The second characteristic of leaders is that they create a purpose. In an earlier segment, we discussed how leaders build motivation by communicating a mission, a sense of direction or even a small set of explicit goals. From the moment they create this direction, all of their actions must support their vision.

Perhaps the most important element of managing from a high purpose is courage. Many times, I have worked with a potential leader who was able to develop a strong sense of purpose but failed to become a leader because at the first hard test of this vision, she blinked. Interestingly, the main issue that such people fail on is one that involves a colleague who is emotionally close to the potential leader and who has used this relationship to become a barrier to change, usually by protecting the status quo. Such a person is acting only in his best interests and not the best interests of the organization. When a leader acts courageously with such a person, the message that goes throughout the organization is that she is serious about this. It's not just another "flavor of the month."

The third element of leadership is determining the stakeholders. Stakeholder is a wonderfully telegraphic term that defines who has a stake in the game, organization, change process, etc. Identifying the stakeholders and understanding their stakes also defines who can hinder or stop the change process as well as those who will be supportive of the change. Defining these constituencies and understanding their core issues begins to suggest strategies to manage the change process.

The fourth element of process leadership is developing and executing tactics that invite the stakeholders into the change process. Recent popular terms describing these processes are participation, involvement, empowerment and engagement. The essential conundrum here is that almost no change processes are democratic. Inviting peoples' participation does not give them a vote or a veto. Excellent leadership is rarely if ever a

> '**Leadership arises out of the heart and out of a personal philosophy about people... Everyone has the responsibility and the duty to influence decision making and to understand the results. Leadership guarantees that decisions will not be arbitrary, secret or closed to questioning. This management is not democratic. Having a say differs from having a vote.**'
>
> **- MAX DePREE**

result of some type of consensus process. On the contrary, such consensual processes often produce the worst type of mediocrity. The leadership skills required to carry out a change process involve knowledge that is almost entirely tacit and thus only available through experience. This is also true of superb management skills. I have a youthful client who is fond of reminding me that I once mentioned to him "I rarely see a good manager under 40."

The fifth and last element of this process model of leadership is the ability of the leader to use the purpose to guide the process to fruition. Strong leadership is necessary to focus, drive and support any change process. For a leader to lead it is necessary for her/him to "work hard and also do the hard work." Successfully managing an organization is a very demanding job that requires more than a full-time commitment. A leader must spend the time doing the work of leading. It is not an accident that many leaders of large organizations have a non-employed spouse who is actively engaged in the ancillary but important social functions of leadership.

The leader must also do the hard work. In general, if a change process is well designed and executed, it is possible to recruit most of the essential people into the process. Every change process produces casualties. Some of these are people who decide they don't care for the new game and move on voluntarily. However, there are people who actively resist and seek to undermine and distort the change process. Such people must be identified and dealt with. As mentioned previously, these are often people who are trading on old relationships to behave in a fashion that is not in the best interests of the organization. It is the responsibility of the leader to confront these people directly and invite them to either change or leave. This is an extremely difficult task and that is why I refer to it as the hard work.

Thinking about leadership in the context of the organization and how to successfully run a change process can provide people a new model to frame how they practice the ongoing development of their organization.

Go To:
Tactical to Strategic (2.8)
Practicing Executive Wisdom (3.18)
What Are the Characteristics of a Great Workplace? (4.6)

3.5

Leadership: A Journey of Self-Awareness

Reading the literature on leadership over many years has been interesting but confusing.

There are too many theories of what leadership is and little direction on how to become a leader. A recent review of leadership identified at least a dozen alternative approaches. In the past couple of years, the confusion has lifted with the insight that there is no perfect leadership style and a shift from trying to define leadership to studying how leaders develop. Let's review the key elements of this more useful approach to leadership.

One pattern is that leaders often emerge from some life crisis that forces them to think long and deep about how they live their lives. This crisis may have been long lasting, such as growing up in poverty, or of short duration, as in having a person close to you die. People who write about these events refer to them as crucibles because of their powerful emotional content. The definition of crucible captures the concept perfectly: a set of circumstances where people are subjected to forces that test them and often make them change. In interviews with leaders, most report such an event or events and then discuss in depth its effects on their lives.

Those who profit from such crucibles show they were able to use this opportunity to examine themselves in a critical manner and reshape themselves into more thoughtful and productive members of society. Self-awareness is the core component central to this analysis and re-direction of one's life. Several years ago, a survey of business leaders indicated that self-awareness was necessary to success in organizational environments, and many business schools are striving to introduce tools and processes to make their graduates more self-reflective.

A crucible is a set of circumstances where people are subjected to forces that test them and often make them change.

Recently, former Medtronic CEO Bill George and his colleagues published an intriguing book titled *True North: Discover Your Authentic Leadership*. Much of this book is summarized in a February 2007 article in the *Harvard Business Review*. Both are reads that lead to considerable reflection.

The most fascinating aspect of this approach is that leaders have a life story. This is not a biography, but the internal story of who they are. This life story, which is under constant revision, defines who they are at their core. This story guides them in how they live their lives. The authors refer to this story as the person's authentic life. To become a leader it is necessary to live in a manner that is authentic to who we are at our very core. This authenticity is shaped by our life experiences and only those of us who examine this experience are aware of who we really are and how we should live our lives. This is pretty existential stuff for business.

I often ask people in interviews to tell me about their lives, and I realized after studying this approach that I am asking them to tell me their life story. Without exception, the people who are leaders have a coherent narrative whereas some people seem to have never developed such a story. Those few without a story seem to be directionless and ineffective in their work lives.

There are several steps in the process of becoming highly self-aware.

Initially, it is essential to use introspective tools to examine your individual leadership development. Here are three of the questions they suggest to begin this self-exploration:

— Which people and experiences in your early life had the greatest impact on you?

— What are your most deeply held values?

— What motivates you extrinsically?

Reflection on these and other questions should clarify your values and principles and help you to act on and live by these values. Such decisions often mean making serious trade-offs, especially about the balance of our personal and professional lives.

Although the life story is the core of this leadership approach, the process continues by introducing additional elements that flow from the story. Some of these are:

— Understanding and balancing your intrinsic and extrinsic motivations

— Building your support team

— Integrating your life by staying grounded

The thrust of the argument is that when these aspects of ourselves are developed, it is possible for us to move into a leadership mode that empowers others to lead.

As a consultant, I have learned that those who improve their performance are open to feedback and willing to examine and alter the basic behavioral style they demonstrate in the workplace. The literature indicates that self-awareness is the first aspect in the process of becoming emotionally intelligent. In organizations, this level of self-reflection seems to spread when respected leaders frame it as process of leadership development. Food for deep thought.

Go To:
Managing: What Are Your Expectations? (2.2)
Courage: Managers into Leaders (2.9)
The executive wisdom segments (3.14 - 18)

In Praise of Peter Drucker

Peter Drucker died on Nov. 11, 2005. He was almost 96 years old and had been writing lucidly until the last several months of his life. I have spent the last 25 years reading management literature, and the person who had the most influence on my thinking about how management should be practiced was Drucker.

He wrote often for the *Wall Street Journal* and the *Harvard Business Review* (HBR), and his articles showed wisdom and common sense. Perhaps one of his best was in the HBR in June 2004: "What makes an effective executive." I have shared it often with clients because it offers great insight into management and leadership at the top.

He began the article by dispelling the popular myth that effective executives have some special personality, often labeled charisma. He notes that executives vary widely on every conceivable personality dimension that anyone can imagine.

However, he noted effective executives follow the same eight practices. They:
Ask what needs to be done.
Ask what is right for the enterprise.
Develop action plans.
Take responsibility for decisions.
Take responsibility for communicating.
Focus on opportunities rather than problems.
Run productive meetings.
Think and say "we" rather than "I."
In these next eight segments, we will look at each of these practices.

The effective executives I have worked with have a keen ability to "sense" the internal needs of the organization. Perhaps the most subtle and powerful tool to sense the organization is that they plug into and read both the content and tone of the "grapevine." A grapevine exists in all organizations and is an accurate index of the concerns and morale of employees. Effective executives understand the value of an executive associate, a person who I often refer to as a "minder." Such a person can greatly extend the influence of an executive by helping him manage scheduling and by becoming a "gatekeeper" who makes sure the right people have

A set of eight key behaviors defines exemplary executive performance.

access to the executive. In addition, the minder can also be a conduit to the grapevine.

I once worked with an executive who was a very early morning person, as was his administrative assistant. The two of them would often have a first cup of coffee together in the morning before anyone else arrived. Sometimes the conversation would be social, but it would often turn to events in the organization and because of her knowledge, sensitivity and ability to read the grapevine, she would provide him with a subtle but powerful view of how things were going. Doing this requires the integrity and skill of both parties because some people try to load this system by providing the executive assistant with their biased view of the organization. However, they worked out these issues and had an excellent working relationship for many years. He often noted that she was able to give him a heads up about important issues much earlier than his chain of command, and he was also able to inject accurate and important information into the grapevine.

I have observed that when new executives come into place, few are "caretakers." They usually adopt one of two tactics; either beginning to change everything immediately or visiting with people, listening to the organization and then beginning to make changes. With the exception of an organization in extremis, the latter tactic is more effective.

The power of spending some serious time sensing the organization is twofold. First, the executive develops keen impressions of the skills and styles of the people who run the organization, as well as a sense of the employees and the culture. One of the interesting things about visiting with people in organizations is that, with enough experience, it is easy to differentiate between those who are genuinely acting in the best interests of the organization and those who are not. The former group will be relied upon for future information and to participate in the change process, whereas the latter will usually show themselves over time as problems. Knowing these distinctions gives the executive a tremendous tactical advantage.

Second, there are many people in organizations who understand the sea they are swimming in (perhaps as many as 40 percent in some companies) and have given serious thought to how to make things better. Identifying and enlisting such people into the change process brings a host of ideas and insights. These impressions and suggestions often share a common set of themes. With this information, the leader can more thoughtfully construct strategy that is in the best interests of the company. When those who have offered such input see their ideas acted upon, they develop ownership in and will support the change process.

Sensing the business and its people and developing direct lines into the grapevine are tactics to ask what needs to be done and require quite high levels of interpersonal skill and integrity.

Go To:
Improving Your Communications Through Active Listening (1.3)
Using Skip-Level Meetings to Sense the Organization (1.14)
Action-Oriented Style (2.6)

3.7

Best For the Company or You — Is It the Same?

Continuing our discussion of the article "What Makes an Effective Executive," one of many fine works by Peter Drucker, we pick up where we left off when we examined his point that leaders "ask what needs to be done."

The second of Drucker's eight characteristics of effective executives is they "ask what is right for the enterprise." This component has two aspects, the first being related to personal integrity.

I have worked with many operating units of large corporations in the manufacturing and service economies. In either case, it is customary for the local executive to spend three to five years running what is usually a profit center before moving to his next assignment. I often refer to such people and their families as "corporate nomads." They always buy a home in a community with the express intention of selling it in several years. This mobility of leadership presents an interesting ethical conundrum for such executives, that choice being that they can make a large number of short-term changes that quickly improve the bottom line of the unit but may have long-term negative consequences, or they can assess the status of the unit and begin to build upon and enhance the accomplishments of their predecessors. Unfortunately, the former strategy is often the one that looks best to corporate headquarters.

This then is the ethical conundrum: to do what is best for the corporation or what is best for oneself. In an ideal world, this dilemma would not occur because the choices are the same. I have been engaged in several "clean-up" operations where the traveling executive made the wrong choice.

Executives must identify the 'core business' and focus as many resources as possible, leveraging the company's best competencies.

After making the decision to act in the best interests of the company, the executive's second task is more profound: determining what is right for the business of the enterprise. A general principle that seems to have produced good results recently — although there are some notable exceptions — is that executives must identify the "core business" and focus as many resources as possible, leveraging the company's best competencies. This strategy has led to the explosion of "outsourcing," which answers the question, "If this is not in your core business and adding value to your products or services, why are you doing it?"

After this core business decision, the issue becomes one of deploying the core business in the marketplace in a fashion that is in the company's best strategic interests. This is perhaps the greatest challenge for executives and their senior staffs. Companies that have managed to carry out this ongoing strategic endeavor tend to be very successful.

For an in-depth analysis of this process, I recommend *Built To Last* by Jim Collins and Jerry Porras. In the book, they define the characteristics of visionary companies and the leaders who guide them to success. The key to the long-term success of companies seems to be the development of a simple but powerful core ideology that consists of core values and a core purpose as well as vividly describing big, audacious goals. If such a conceptual framework is lived by leadership, it appears to unleash the potential of many people throughout the organization. Needless to say, this is a complex, ongoing process.

The fascinating thing about these strategic successes is how fragile they can be even after many years of successful practice. A case in point is HP, a company with a powerful and long-term culture of success. A few years ago, they brought in Carly Fiorina, an outside CEO who proceeded to make a bitterly opposed acquisition and then adopted the culture of the acquired company by promoting executives from that organization into leadership positions. Subsequently, after what has been reported as a series of tumultuous board meetings, she was summarily discharged. Now, her successor is deeply engaged in rebuilding virtually the entire culture of the organization. In a few short years, the ousted executive managed to completely disassemble what had been one of the most successful corporate cultures in American business.

Watching such examples of poor leadership has caused me to revise a basic belief about how people run organizations. That belief is that all people in senior management positions will do what is best for the organization. In my own consulting practice, I have occasionally worked with companies where senior executives, although they speak their concern for the health of the organization, rarely act in a manner that supports that concern. I have concluded from these experiences, as well as the experiences of working with executives who do act in the best interests of their companies, that for organizations to be successful over time, many people at the top of the organization must be committed to its best interests and continuously acting in support of that commitment.

Go To:
Beware: Change Imposed is Change Opposed (1.9)
Engagement and Decision Making (2.5)
Values of the Ethical Manager (2.12)

3.8

SMART Action Plans Help Direct Work Toward Goals

Continuing our discussion of the article "What Makes an Effective Executive" by Peter Drucker, we look at his third point: Leaders "develop action plans."

One can hardly underestimate the value of explicit actions plans. The Chinese have an aphorism, "If you don't know where you are going, any road will take you there." Action plans are the road maps that focus the collective activities of groups of people (such as companies) and measure progress.

Understanding this, I am often amazed that many employees don't have a clue about the goals of their departments and their company, and most do not have any kind of performance plan that they regularly review with their supervisors. Here is an area where companies can markedly improve their productivity as well as their peoples' morale. People love to succeed, and if leaders develop thoughtful plans, they give people focus, provide feedback toward progress and offer a source of personal and organizational satisfaction.

The key question then is what constitutes an effective action plan, objective or goal? The answer is action plans that are SMART. Smart means Simple, Measurable, Attainable Responsibility is assigned and Timeframes (deadlines) are defined. Let's examine each of these attributes in turn.

Simple is the foremost in importance. People cannot commit to actions that they do not understand. The more complex an action plan, the less likely people will understand it and commit to it. Some years ago, I read a book by Richard Schonberger called *World Class Manufacturing*. According to Schonberger, the three principles of world-class manufacturing are simplify, simplify, simplify.

Simplification is one of the greatest challenges in the modern workplace. Most people love complexity; technology drives complexity and it is easy to make things and ideas complex. Making them simple is very difficult. One of my favorite maxims is, "How do you eat an elephant?" The answer is one bite at a time (and where you take the first bite is very important).

> # The Chinese have an aphorism, 'If you don't know where you are going, any road will take you there.'

The French mathematician Pierre-Simon LaPlace said if you cannot measure something, you cannot understand it. Good measurement is an effective way to bring discipline to a company. It provides individual and collective progress measures that not only energize performance but also provide opportunities to readjust the process to produce a better result. Good measurement need not be complex, but it does need to be frequent.

The key to great action plans is that they are neither too hard nor too easy. If they are too easy, people develop a false sense of accomplishment and their performance erodes. If too difficult, people cannot succeed, are demoralized and often quit trying. The key to "raising the bar" without either of these effects is to raise performance standards incrementally. If this is done with skilled managing and coaching, the performance of people and groups can improve markedly.

Who is responsible? Let's all stand in a circle and point left. Harry Truman had a sign on his desk in the White House that read, "The buck stops here." The essence of this attribute is that responsibility must be assigned to an individual. Not assigning responsibility provides no mechanism to define who has the buck.

Assigning responsibility to a group is a more tricky decision. If the group is in fact a functional team, something that I rarely see in companies in spite of all the rhetoric about teams, it will be accomplished. But in general, it is better to put a person "on the dime" and then he becomes your "go-to guy."

Americans work to deadlines. In fact, analysis of patterns of work show that as the deadline approaches, the intensity of work accelerates. Consider then how important timelines are to carrying out the performance of work. People are very shrewd at allocating their time with regard to the deadlines they must meet. Therefore, managers must be wise in the manner that they build timeframes to maximize the performance of people and groups.

SMART action plans provide a tool to engage people into helping them define the conditions of their work as well as setting up explicit performance standards that encourage ever better performance. When people accomplish these goals, it creates a natural context to provide timely, accurate feedback and reward successful performance.

Go To:
KISSing and Chunking: A Magical Method for
Better Communications (1.4)
Managing Better Meetings (1.8)
Engagement and Decision Making (2.5)

Good Leaders Take Responsibility for Communication

In the last segment, we examined Peter Drucker's point that leaders "develop action plans." Continuing our discussion of his article about "What Makes an Effective Executive," we discuss his next point: "Leaders take responsibility for communicating." Because good communication is so central to organizational performance, we are going to spend a couple of segments on this topic.

"The better informed people are, the better they perform" is a fundamental principle of good management. However, assessments of various types of people in organizations always show that people at every level in the organization believe that communication could be better. Assuming that we all believe more communication is better, why isn't it done more effectively? Communication is a skill that, like management, improves with practice and when it is principle based. Here are some fundamental principles about how good communication should occur.

Active is always better than passive. Leading and managing people are active processes. Active mechanisms always work better than passive. For example, many managers are proud of their open-door policies; when we talk to employees they are underwhelmed by such passive practices. Open-door policies do not invite people to communicate, and the evidence is that most people, especially the reasonable people you want to hear from, do not use them.

> ## Each of us has had the experience of making a seemingly innocent remark that engenders an enormously negative reaction (husbands take note).

Keep it short and simple (KISS). I believe it was Mark Twain who wrote, "If I had more time, I would have written a shorter letter." Many people seem to equate the quantity of communications with the quality. In reality, the reverse is the case. Psychologists refer to a characteristic called cognitive efficiency, which describes peoples' ability to identify the core elements in communication and then structure these elements in a way that makes it easy to recall and act upon them. This phenomenon is called chunking. Consider if I ask you to carry out three tasks versus asking you to carry out 17 tasks. Which are you more likely to understand, remember and execute?

Focus – focus – focus. Over the years, I have learned that effective people and effective organizations do a few things very well. This is closely related to "KISS," but important enough that it deserves distinction. The easiest way to make people and organizations fail is to put too many tasks on their plate. This means that the resources, effort or whatever will be dispersed and used to the least effect. Many people who write about leadership note that leaders are very skilled at mobilizing and motivating people by focusing them on a small set of goals that are important.

Use the appropriate channel of communication. The primary transmission and reception channels are verbal — both written and spoken — and non-verbal — our actions and our body language.

Employees respect people who walk their talk, whether they are peers, supervisors, managers or executives. This is the ultimate test of integrity for many people. Do you do what you say you are going to do? I call it the say/do ratio, and employees are better watchers of manager behavior than many people comprehend.

The issue of communication channels also is related to the preferred mode of transmission and reception of those you work with every day. Consider the differences between a person-to-person conversation, a phone visit, a voice mail, an e-mail and a fax. Each is effective or ineffective for some types of communications and with some types of people.

Have you developed personal and organizational strategies to maximize the strengths and minimize the shortcomings of each of these modes?

Manage the content/feeling dimension. Many managers fail to fully understand that all communication has two inter-related dimensions: content and feeling. The content part of the communication is the "what," the denotative, objective content. This part of the message is often perceived to be relatively unambiguous. But the other part of the communication, the emotional or feeling dimension, the "how," often determines the effects of the communication on the receiver.

Over time, I have learned that what people think is very important, but what they feel almost always trumps what they think. Each of us knows this from the experience of making a seemingly innocent remark that engenders an enormously negative reaction (husbands take note).

We also know that the power of the negative far outweighs the power of the positive. The sting of a thoughtless remark can be long lasting. Understanding the power of the feeling content of all the forms of communication gives us a better understanding of how to motivate people.

As we strive to improve our communication styles, it is important to pay attention to the how of communication as well as the what. In the next segment, we will examine what employees need to know.

Go To:
KISSing and Chunking: A Magical Method for Better Communications (1.4)
Courage: Managers into Leaders (2.9)
If You See a Bathroom, Use It! (5.2)

It's Important to Give Employees Vital Information

Continuing the discussion of Peter Drucker's article, "What Makes an Effective Executive," begun in previous segments, we pick up from looking at "how" to communicate to look now at "what" employees need to know.

"Open communication" assumes that "the better informed people are, the better they function." This is an easy principle to understand but a difficult one to practice. If organizations tried to keep everyone informed about everything there would be no time to do any work. Thus, it is necessary to determine what critical information employees must have to perform their jobs in an optimal manner.

Keeping people well informed so they can successfully perform their jobs is a continuing and critical management responsibility. In reviewing the content of numerous conversations and sensing sessions with employees, it is possible to define three major chunks of information that people report will enhance their job performance. These are:

• **Specific knowledge of the job.** Clearly, the more a person knows about her job, the more likely she is to perform well. In today's rapidly changing work environment, most employees realize their future job security and potential for advancement depend heavily on maintaining and enhancing their competence. It is essential that employees' have the information-based skills necessary to perform the job to the best of their abilities.

Because personal competence is related so directly to productivity, the issue of job knowledge is one that both the employee and her immediate supervisor share responsibility for managing. This means the ability of the manager to be an effective coach becomes ever more important. Experience shows the management style of the first-level manager is the essential ingredient to quality and productivity. Often, employee performance is substandard and some even fail simply because we do not help them to succeed by assuring they receive adequate information about their jobs and feedback about their job performance. Most employees report that they receive insufficient feedback from their immediate supervisors.

• **An understanding of how each job fits into the process of carrying**

Without strategic management, an organization will continue to do what it always has done.

out work. As work becomes more complex and requires people to work together in more cooperative ways, the importance of each person understanding how their job fits into the process of building a product or delivering a service is more apparent.

The understanding of employees that they have internal customers within the organization allows people to examine how they help and hinder each other's work. The quality of the working relationships within groups of employees responsible for a product or service is necessary to ensure quality.

We know that sub-optimization, a tendency to do the job in a manner that makes it easier for the individual without consideration about how it hinders the work of others, has an extremely negative effect on quality. This phenomenon has its most negative effects when companies have departments that behave like vertical chimneys where there is little cross communication at the levels where work gets done.

In contrast, research on productive and innovative organizations shows that excellent lateral communications, especially across boundaries such as departments, is fundamental to quality and productivity. Introducing the concept that employees have internal customers is essential to addressing the lateral communication and cooperation. Where it is applied with attention to involving employees, it produces impressive gains in quality and productivity.

• **A clear understanding of the "big picture."** The management of specific knowledge of the job and an understanding of the process of how work gets done can be thought of as tactical management. The third type of information employees need defines a significant component of strategic management.

Without strategic management, an organization will continue to do what it always has done. Employees often function in a vacuum of information about the overall values and goals of the organization, the "big picture." Formulating this overall strategy, whether for a working unit, a department or a total organization, is central to the strategic management of any organization.

Strategic management must teach people in an organization to begin questioning the very natural human tendency to do things the way they always have done them. It is at this point in communications practice that we make the shift from management to leadership.

An excellent definition of the distinction between the two is that management is getting work done through people and leadership is producing positive change. Clearly, in the turbulent organizational environments that exist today, the importance of leadership is more critical than it was in a more stable past.

Strategic management consists primarily of explicitly defining and clearly communicating the basic purposes of the organization. Formulating these basic characteristics for the organization is the major task of successful change masters.

Perhaps the most essential of these strategic elements is making sure that a periodic review of the basic business model is carried out and shared with everyone in the organization.

Such a process invites everyone to assess the viability of the business model and identify external and internal issues that may lead to a reconsideration of the model. In turbulent business environments, the ability to carry out such a strategic activity is an important ingredient to the organization's ability to survive and thrive.

Clearly, communication is not as simple as we often believe. Knowing what and how to communicate is an essential set of cognitive, emotional and behavioral skills for the manager-leader.

If we believe that manager-leaders have enormous influence over those who look upward to them in the organization, then modeling these essentials will have a deeply felt and positive effect on the organization.

Also, communicating that everyone must contribute to the quality of communications in an organization begins to distribute responsibility for this critical function.

Go To:
Coaching to Improve Performance (1.6)
Driving Quality Improvements with the Internal Customer Model (1.17)
Tactical to Strategic (2.8)

Decide the Best Method Before Making an Important Decision

In previous segments, we considered some concrete aspects of effective communication. Another of the eight practices of effective executives is that they take responsibility for decisions.

The easiest way to assess the managerial philosophy of an organization is to develop an understanding of how the organization makes decisions. In an earlier segment (2.5), we discussed the four major types of decision making — authoritarian, authoritative, consultative and consensual — and noted that managers should have all four in their repertoires. Each is applicable to a different kind of situation: authoritarian for emergencies, authoritative for situations where increasing the skill and knowledge of workers is essential, consultative when the goal is to engage people in the process of work and consensual when the goal is to spread the decision deeper into the organization.

Trust is another essential ingredient to the optimal functioning of a company. Executives and managers must trust each other or communication breaks down. Workers throughout an organization must trust their leaders, especially their immediate manager, or they will not give their best performance on a daily basis. Customers must trust the company or they will not buy the organization's products and services.

One definition of leadership is understanding and using power wisely. However, thinking about power is troubling because it is difficult to define just what power is in a positive fashion. Certainly, the use of power is obvious in a reduction in force, a pay freeze or the separation of an employee. But these examples only provide specific situations where the results are generally negative. Perhaps such easily recalled examples are the reason discussions of power are difficult.

Weaving the concepts of power, decision making and trust together, we can understand how executives and managers can exercise power wisely to build trust within the organization. The key to this understanding is an in-depth knowledge of decision making and the experience to make good decisions about how to make decisions.

It is reasonable to define the management of people as having two

The easiest way to assess the managerial philosophy of a company is to develop an understanding of how the organization makes decisions.

major components: communication and decision making. Decision making is a specific example of communication. Nothing communicates more quickly or emotionally than a negative decision that affects a large number of people within an organization. Perhaps this is the reason the causal relationship between decision making and trust is not better examined and understood.

Decision making is the most visible example of the use of power in an organization and understanding it can be an important way to understand how to use the power of a managerial or executive position to build or destroy trust.

In authoritarian decisions, all the power rests in the hands of the decider. Power corrupts and absolute power corrupts absolutely. An example of this is the newly promoted manager who is burning to make changes and is hurrying to use her newly minted decision-making authority to solve problems she has been looking at for some time. Or, consider the often-noted micro-manager who becomes involved in decision making at a level of detail that infuriates workers by making them feel stupid. In both cases, good intentions to change situations for the better have opposite effects and become trust busters. The core problem in these situations is the manager's lack of understanding of using power wisely and the absence of some form of counter-control within the system. There is no safe way for people to push back to influence the behavior of the manager.

Consider the contrasting effects in the case of the unwise use of consensual decision making. In this instance, the manager inappropriately hands off the authority for decisions to a person or group and the decision essentially runs off the rails by becoming authoritarian, which seems to be the default position for people unschooled in the types of decision making. An inappropriate decision badly done then has to be reversed, often by someone above the manager who made the hand-off, thus creating negative effects in all three parties directly involved in the decision. In this situation, the decision-making power was diffused is a manner that sets the stage for problems to develop.

Executive function is the clear definition of who has what responsibility for decision making. It acknowledges that when individuals have such authority, there is less likelihood of problems developing, particularly if the person is knowledgeable about decision types. It also recognizes that group decision making is subject to forces that are sometimes difficult to understand and address.

Interestingly enough, when conversant with the decision-making continuum, most people recognize the risks of over-using authoritarian and consensual decision making and intuitively understand that building a successful authoritative style is a necessary condition to moving to consultative decision making and employee engagement.

Clearly, the performance of organizations can be enhanced by assuring that key people thoroughly understand how thoughtful decision making can be a powerful trust builder.

Go To:
Engagement and Decision Making (2.5)
How Managers Fail (2.11)
Practicing Executive Wisdom (3.18)

Focus on Opportunities and Run Good Meetings

In this segment we will look at two of the eight characteristics Peter Drucker identifies in his article, "What makes an effective executive:" Focus on opportunities and run good meetings.

Everyone in the workplace knows the reward for doing good work is getting more work. If leadership is motivating people to perform, then a part of that function must be creating situations that energize and encourage people, not discourage them. How many people function in work environments where the total focus is on solving immediate problems? Over time this becomes tiring and de-motivating.

In another segment, I discuss the concept of mentally framing perceptions and how this affects our performance. Effective executives understand that framing events as opportunities is more motivating than being on the treadmill of solving problems. They also understand that assigning the best people to the biggest opportunities has a much greater impact on organizational performance than continuously putting talented people on problems. This seems like a simple idea, but it is striking how many managers fall into the trap of driving their workforces exclusively with crisis management.

As work becomes more complex and requires more communication and cooperation among participants, the importance of effective meetings becomes more critical to organizational productivity. Part of a leader's function is to carry out effective meetings, yet most lack the skills to do so. Here are some simple principles for good meeting management.

An effective meeting must have a leader. Meetings often degenerate because no one has taken responsibility for managing the process of meeting. It is the duty of a leader to take responsibility for managing the process. This means following the "be prepared" motto and assuring that certain conditions exist.

A good meeting first must have a clear purpose. Are we meeting at 9 a.m. on Monday because we have always done so? People prefer to attend meetings that have either clear goals or where the first item on the agenda is to formulate clear goals. If all meeting participants asked the

Effective executives understand that assigning the best people to the biggest opportunities has a much greater impact on organizational performance than continuously putting talented people on problems.

question "why are we here?" and no satisfactory answer was apparent, many meetings would immediately discontinue. The development of explicit goals gives direction to any endeavor.

Meetings need an explicit set of ground rules, principles of how we will behave and treat each other. Explicit expectations can greatly enhance the productivity of a meeting. Here is an example of a set of ground rules developed by a team that consisted of managers and employees:

- Be/start on time, stay on task and end on time.
- Commit to attend and conduct effective regularly scheduled agenda-driven meetings.
- Be courteous and show respect for others' ideas by letting everyone contribute in turn.
- Solve problems; don't place blame. Another important element of a successful meeting is an agenda. Once clear goals are formulated, an agenda comes easily. The agenda makes explicit the topics, their order and the time allocated for each. Good agendas rarely have more than five to nine items. A good way to kill a meeting is to make the agenda too long or too complex.

In a situation where there have been serious meeting management problems, it is appropriate to assign times to the agenda. It is also important that the agenda include a section that summarizes the results of the meeting and defines work assignments as well as the time and place of the next meeting. Assuring a stable time and place will enhance attendance.

The goals, ground rules and agenda provide tools for the leader to manage the meeting process. People respond positively to simple statements such as "we are off task" or "please remember ground rule no. 3" or "it is time to move on to item four." Such gentle reminders can keep a meeting flowing smoothly.

The final conditions for a successful meeting are membership and size. A committee, group or team cannot accomplish its purpose if the appropriate people are not in attendance. Meetings work much better when they have enough people but not too many. In most cases, the optimal number is five to nine. Groups above 10 rarely work together well. Larger groups need an effective sub-committee structure to function well. Meeting management is a skill that improves when it is based on a set of principles. The most effective method to improve the quality of a meeting is to analyze the meeting's problems and discuss how to resolve them as a group.

For example, the leadership role could be rotated so each participant had responsibility for meeting management for an agreed-upon number of meetings. This gets everyone in touch with how difficult it can be to run an effective meeting.

Another useful tool is to take several minutes at the end of the meeting and do a round-robin on how the meeting went. The key to better meeting management is to appreciate that meetings need to be managed.

Go To:
Managing Better Meetings (1.8)
If You See a Bathroom, Use It! (5.2)
Self-Talk to Success or Failure? (5.4)

Effective Executives Say 'We,' not 'I,' in the Workplace

We have been looking at the characteristics outlined in Peter Drucker's article "What makes an effective executive," and this segment examines the last of the eight characteristics: Effective executives say "we," not "I."

Running an organization requires a substantial portion of self-confidence. Tentative managers and leaders are perceived as weak and are not effective in getting work done through people. However, we have recently seen the tragic results of hubris and egotism in several large corporations. As in so many things in life, the key is to find the right balance between extremes; would that our politicians would heed this advice.

Drucker notes in forceful terms that leaders rarely use "I," especially in front of employees. Instead they often use "we," and this serves to communicate to subordinates that their contribution to the organization is valued. In general, effective managers use language that communicates to their employees in a respectful manner. It is always interesting to note how managers introduce employees and how they engage them in conversation. If you do this long enough, it is clear that tentative, weak managers are insecure and that egotists are likewise insecure. The reason that such managers demean others is that it gives them a sense of superiority, however false.

Looking deeper into managerial communications, one of the biggest trust busters in an organization happens when a manager fails to appropriately credit an employee(s) for good work or, even worse, takes the credit for himself. In his book, *Good to Great*, Jim Collins notes that effective leaders give away as much credit as is possible and take as much of the blame on themselves as is reasonable.

Employees detest managers that "hang them out to dry" when mistakes are made. An effective manager instead uses the mistake to create an opportunity to learn how to get it right the next time. How managers communicate day-to-day sends strong messages to employees as well as setting expectations that affect performance. Employees and consultants use this as a tool to measure and infer what a person's management style may be and how it will affect them.

Correlated with what could rightfully be called realistic humility is an

Drucker offers a bonus
No. 9: Listen first, speak last.

independence of titles. Many organizations are choking on excessive numbers of titles and it is interesting that the most insecure and poorest performing people seem to cling to their titles and insist on being addressed using the title. Employees respect titles and appreciate the work that it took to attain the position, but they resent having the title used in a fashion that makes them feel as if they are second-class citizens.

I began this series by introducing Drucker's eight practices of effective executives. Each of these we have examined in some depth. Effective executives:

- Ask what needs to be done
- Ask what is right for the enterprise
- Develop action plans
- Take responsibility for decisions
- Take responsibility for communicating
- Focus on opportunities rather than problems
- Run productive meetings
- Think and say "we" rather than "I"

Drucker offers a bonus No. 9: Listen first, speak last.

It is important to note that several of these patterns of behavior should also be in the skill sets of effective supervisors and managers.

Leadership, according to Warren Bennis, has four profound effects. Leaders behave in a manner that creates an environment where:

- People feel significant
- Learning and competence matter
- People are part of a community
- Work-life is exciting

This is a very high bar to reach. How many of us can truly say that we work in such an environment?

Go To:
Courage: Managers into Leaders (2.9)
What are Your Motivators and Demotivators? (4.5)
If You See a Bathroom, Use It! (5.2)

Executive Wisdom: Context

Periodically we experience an upsurge of unethical actions by executives in organizations. The consequences of these actions are not only self-defeating but often have catastrophic effects on others. We are again in one of these periods. This upsurge of unethical behavior always catalyzes much writing, some of it good, about topics such as leadership and wisdom.

Little thought or voice is given to the challenges of running an organization in this fast-paced global economy. This lack of context renders most of the information "talking heads" produce absurd at best and misleading at worst. It is impossible to examine leadership issues without understanding the current context in which executives in companies of all sizes must function.

It is a truism that we live in a world of increasing complexity and rapid change. In general, it is fair to say that most things happen much faster than they did just a few years ago. Some time ago, my fax machine fell silent, and then my voice mail and now every morning there are many e-mails, some from people who expect an immediate response. Several executives I know have become captives of their Blackberries (or are they razzberries?). Some state legislatures have passed laws to make "texting" (is this a noun or a verb) illegal while operating a motor vehicle.

So, a look at context. The modern corporation has its origins in the industrial revolution. Before that time, with the exception of armies, most products and services were produced by what today we would call cottage industries, mom and pop shops. Some say the Italians invented the future when they invented banking. Others say the English invented the future by building a global business empire, with some help from the Royal Navy, based on manufacturing.

The industrial revolution forced organizations to bring ever-larger numbers of people together to produce products. Thus was born the hierarchical organization that we know today. This organizational structure was largely birthed by three men: Henry Ford who introduced mass production; Frederick Taylor who systematized jobs into standardized tasks (thus making them boring); and Alfred Sloan who wove many small auto companies together to create General Motors.

This typical hierarchical organization does some things very well, but its bureaucratic structure is inherently resistant to change. However, organizations must be hierarchical because it is the most efficient method of allocating responsibility and authority that anyone has ever conceived. Misguided change initiatives such as "self-directed work teams" have demonstrated that a chain of responsibility is necessary.

'Good judgment comes from experience, and a lot of that comes from bad judgment.'

- WILL ROGERS

During the 20th century we saw the recession of the agricultural economy (typical worker: farmer) and the ascendance and recession of both the industrial (typical worker: laborer) and service economies (typical worker: clerk) and the emergence of an information-driven economy (typical worker: technician). The older three sectors of the economy are being bifurcated by the information economy into high information-high compensation and low information-low compensation economies. You can see this clearly by looking at where jobs are being created and destroyed. Work in the first world is moving rapidly from muscle to mental.

As the information economy accelerated and global competition became an issue, large corporations began a decades-long process of "downsizing," mostly by introducing automation and by streamlining to improve their competitiveness. Hundreds of thousands of mostly industrial jobs were eliminated. Thus began what some have called the "turbulent economy" that continuously and simultaneously destroys and creates jobs. A remarkable characteristic of the American economy is that on average it has added a net gain of about 200,000 jobs to the economy each month for the past 20 years while destroying millions. Were any of you wondering why modern life is stressful?

It is axiomatic that the most important process in organizations is communication. Abundant evidence shows that companies that move information rapidly, particularly sideways, are more productive and innovative than those that do not. Interestingly enough, the more complex an organization (locations, functions, layers, etc.) becomes, the more difficult it is to communicate clearly and to "sense" the ongoing activities of the organization. Executives rely heavily on financial measures because these are currently the best way to gauge the ongoing performance of the organization. Unfortunately, such measures often do not operate rapidly enough nor do they provide innovative ideas on how to make productive change.

In most organizations, too many decisions are made too high in the organization. Paradoxically, such decisions often are made with incomplete or inaccurate information because of organizational complexity. Hence, the organizational structures that have served so well in the past now act as barriers to effective communication and decision making. Increase this by some orders of magnitude by changing the context from local to global. No wonder CEOs of multi-national corporations have about a five-year tenure. It's not easy to be wise when size, speed, complexity and cultural differences introduce turbulence. So, what is executive wisdom and how can we cultivate it?

Go To:
Organizations and Management (2.1)
The Power of Information (2.3)
Organizations Come in Three Varieties (3.21)

The Information Continuum

In the previous segment, we placed the challenges of organizational leadership into the context of the increasing speed and complexity of the contemporary global business environment. As wisdom is integral to leadership and is inherently a cognitive process, we must understand the information continuum that begins with data and ends with wisdom. Understanding the data – information – knowledge – wisdom continuum is fundamental to our discussion of wisdom.

Data is the basic building block of the information continuum and binary data is the most basic type of data. The idea that we can use the simple fact of a switch being on or off has led to the explosion of information technology. One key quest in data processing is to reduce large amounts of data to information.

Information most easily is defined by what the human mind can learn, recall and act upon. Cognitively efficient people store and retrieve information in "chunks" and that the maximum size of a chunk is seven plus/minus two. Thus, if you want to have others remember what you say and write, follow the KISSing and chunking rule. Keep It Short and Simple and make sure that your chunks do not exceed the magical seven plus/minus two. Peter Drucker further refines the definition of information by stating, "Information is data endowed with relevance and purpose. Converting data into information thus requires knowledge."

Excellent communicators understand these principles intuitively. Looking across history, it is impressive to see how many powerful documents are organized in this fashion. One fascinating aspect of this principle is that the disciplined human mind can store and retrieve vast amounts of information if it is organized hierarchically. I once took an outstanding course from a genetics professor who taught the whole semester without a single note. He would come into class, sit on the lab bench, light a cigarette and talk with us. The lectures were intimate, well organized and so fascinating that I remember him and much of the material all these years later.

Now journey with me into the realm of epistemology and let me share ideas about knowledge with you. Knowledge comes in three flavors: explicit, tacit and scientific. Explicit knowledge is knowledge that has been or can be articulated, codified and stored in media. It can be readily

> ## 'Information is data endowed with relevance and purpose. Converting data into information thus requires knowledge.'
>
> ### - PETER DRUCKER

transmitted to others. Explicit or content knowledge is textbook knowledge. It is useful to think of it as "what" knowledge and it is the basic operating material of formal educational systems.

By definition, tacit knowledge is knowledge that people carry in their minds and is, therefore, difficult to access. Often, people are not aware of the knowledge they possess or how it can be valuable to others. Tacit knowledge is considered more valuable because it provides context for people, places, ideas and experiences. Effective transfer of tacit knowledge generally requires extensive personal contact and trust. It is reasonable to think of tacit knowledge as "how" knowledge.

To fully understand the difference between explicit and tacit knowledge, consider the fate of a recent college graduate in an information-driven job such as engineering, finance or marketing. Such a person leaves school with a large fund of explicit knowledge. But consider how long it takes them to learn "how" to do the job, to master the tacit knowledge that cannot be learned in the classroom and is most easily learned with guidance of a skilled and experienced mentor. Interestingly, much of this tacit knowledge is intuitive and thus has an emotional intelligence content.

The third type of knowledge is scientific knowledge. Science, in the broadest sense, refers to any system of knowledge that attempts to model objective reality. In a more restricted sense, science refers to a system of acquiring knowledge based on the scientific method, as well as to the organized body of knowledge gained through such research. Scientific knowledge can be thought of as "why" knowledge and gets us closer to the issue of ultimate verities.

Comparing management and medicine is useful to help understand these types of knowledge. Medicine is a scientifically driven art. This means that the science can be learned in a conventional manner, but there is enormous tacit knowledge that makes the difference between a mediocre practitioner and an expert. Medical schools recognize the importance of tacit knowledge in the manner they train physicians. In physician training, huge amounts of time are spent on-the-job under the close supervision of experienced mentors.

Management is also an art, but it is a principle-driven art. Business schools have not fully integrated this knowledge into their curricula; far too much time is being focused on the content of business rather than developing on-the-job opportunities for students to work closely under the guidance of an experienced mentor honing their tacit knowledge-based skills. In defense of business schools, it is far easier to do this when you have captive training organizations such as hospitals where your practitioners work. It may also be that there is less agreement about what constitutes effective management practice. Medicine has an easier time as they have the solid bedrock of "caring for people's health."

The next segment considers what wisdom is and how it develops.

Go To:
Coaching to Improve Performance (1.6)
The Power of Information (2.3)
Harness the Power of Mentoring in Your Business (3.20)

Executive Wisdom Involves Balancing Knowledge

In the two previous segments, we discussed executive wisdom in the context of the global economy and reviewed the basic natures of data, information and knowledge.

The nature of wisdom is in equal parts philosophical and empirical. One philosophical definition is as follows: Wisdom is the ability, developed through experience, insight and reflection, to discern truth and exercise good judgment. Wisdom is sometimes conceptualized as an especially well-developed form of common sense. It is distinct from the cognitive abilities measured by standardized intelligence tests. Wisdom is often considered a trait that can be developed by experience, but not taught. The status of wisdom as a virtue is recognized in cultural, philosophical and religious sources.

After several years of consulting experience, I noticed that some managers could make any management tool work, whereas others seemed incapable of using the simplest tool without its application causing problems. A thoughtless manager can use any management tool, regardless of how principled and well designed, to make situations for employees worse rather than better.

It took me some time to fully appreciate that this was entirely about the presence or absence of certain types of tacit knowledge. The effective manager intuitively understands that "how" (tacitly) the tool is applied is the key to its effectiveness. To support this contention, I have occasionally recommended what I thought to be an effective tool for a manager only to return to the organization later to learn how it had been misapplied and caused rather than solved problems. These experiences drive home the importance of tacit knowledge in working with people.

Understanding that tacit knowledge is an essential ingredient in the above definition of executive wisdom further strengthened my belief in the salience of the emotional component of management and leadership. An interesting hypothesis for managers and potential leaders to ponder is that "in most situations involving human beings, emotion trumps reason." I have been reflecting on this concept for some years now and it further reinforces the idea that people are essentially emotional creatures.

Antonio Damasio, a former faculty member at the University of Iowa

> # Wisdom is often considered to be a trait that can be developed by experience, but not taught.

College of Medicine, wrote an extremely provocative book several years ago titled *Descartes Error*. Rene Descartes was the philosopher and theologian who in his proof of God stated, "cogito ergo sum," "I think therefore I exist." Damasio believes that Descartes got it exactly wrong; what makes us uniquely human is not reason, but emotion. His lucid and compelling discussion of this hypothesis is a ripping good read.

The behavior of people can be thought of as having three essential ingredients: cognition, emotion and action. These interact with each other in complex fashions to produce the wide range of behavior we observe every day. Given that tacit knowledge is often about the ability to read and manage our own and the emotional behavior of others, one can understand the central importance of human emotion. A wise person then must have a finely tuned understanding of the interaction between thought and emotion and its consequences, particularly in communication.

For a dramatic comparison, contrast the styles of two recent presidents: Ronald Reagan and Jimmy Carter. When Reagan spoke, people felt uplifted and energized whereas Carter always presented in a manner that spoke only to our problems and not our possibilities. How future historians will evaluate these two presidents may well hinge on their abilities to cast very different emotional pictures in their communications and thus their power as leaders.

Go To:
A Multi-Dimensional View of Motivation and Morale (4.1)
What Is Your Attitude Toward Work? (4.2)
Self-Talk to Success or Failure? (5.4)

Defining Executive Wisdom

Wisdom has both philosophical and empirical definitions. A workable empirical definition of wisdom is the application of tacit knowledge in pursuing the common good and requiring a balance of intra-, inter- and extra-personal interests and environmental circumstances. In the last segment, we examined the importance of tacit knowledge in the development of executive wisdom.

The common good is a term that can refer to several different concepts. In the popular meaning, the common good describes a specific good that is shared and beneficial for all (or most) members of a given community. Based on this definition, it is reasonable to project that the common good in executive wisdom is focused on the organization and the larger community that the organization exists within.

In general, leaders are well read, often avidly in history, and have a strategic understanding of the inter-relatedness of the various constituent parts of systems. This level of knowledge is necessary to even begin to comprehend the common good. The chamber of commerce in many communities enacts community leadership programs to provide the opportunity for incipient leaders to understand the various elements of their communities and how these elements affect each other. The basic assumption of these programs is to create a context that invites participants to perceive the grand contextual sweep of events and systems and is an essential ingredient of wisdom.

Working in organizations, I am struck by how comfortable most people are staying in the details. Often, many people cannot see the forest for the trees but cannot see the trees for the leaves. There is a comfort in staying in the details that cannot be found in strategic issues where the central and critical characteristic is usually ambiguity. I was with a group of senior managers in a manufacturing plant where the organizational solution to the problem seemed obvious but most of the managers could not see outside their silo and therefore could not comprehend a solution that involved the collaborative actions of most of them. It was as if the strong individual responsibilities made it difficult to even imagine a tactic that necessitated shared responsibility. We finally found a solution to the core barrier to organizational improvement by getting them to think of the organization not in terms of a traditional pyramid but rather a set of overlapping Venn diagrams where the shared issues were at the intersections.

Apart from comprehension, perhaps one of the greatest challenges to the effective operation of complex systems is the activity of single-issue advocates who often perceive their issue as the only one of import. They do not understand how their lack of understanding of the complexities can cause the enactment of a single issue to cascade in harmful ways throughout a system. Each of the previously mentioned managers was working very hard to do the best for her part of the organization, but because their actions were uncoordinated, the results were dramatically suboptimal for the organization. Such single-minded advocacy fails utterly to comprehend or re-adjust to the law of unintended consequences.

'Wisdom is not knowledge, but lies in the use we make of knowledge.'

- N. SRI RAM

Thus, to even understand the meaning of the common good it is necessary to understand fully the context within which the person or organization exists. The Germans have a charming term, zeitgeist, or spirit of the times, that signifies this larger cultural context.

Peter Drucker often spoke of the necessity of reflection by persons in positions of leadership. The ability to step outside of one's perceptions, biases and experiences and to reflect on all the various aspects of a complex system is the first step toward what many who write about wisdom regard as an essential function, discernment. The Latin root of this term means "to separate by sifting." Discernment then is a powerful cognitive skill that involves the acquisition of a wide breadth of knowledge, both explicit and tacit, and the systematic analysis of this knowledge to yield a wise judgment.

Go To:
Why Ethical Behavior Is Profitable (2.10)
Leadership Is an Important Organizational
Performance Driver (3.1)

Practicing Executive Wisdom

Thus far in this set we have examined the context of wisdom, the relationship of wisdom to explicit and tacit knowledge, the nature of wisdom and the nature of executive wisdom. All of this is of little value without some discussion of the uses of wisdom.

The central difference between wisdom and executive wisdom is that executive wisdom comes with considerable power. One way to think of leadership is as an exercise in the wise use of power. Thoughtful executives must comprehend at both emotional and cognitive levels that their decisions can have profound effects, for good or ill, on the lives of the persons in their organizations, as well as have considerable impact on the people, communities and organizations on the boundaries of their companies.

Even first-level managers can have enormous influence on the lives of their direct reports. The termination of an employee, for whatever reason, will have a serious effect on the person and his or her family as well as other employees. Thus, the various checks and balances within organizations to prevent such a decision from becoming routine and casual.

Because of the egalitarian nature of our culture, Americans are not comfortable with the concept of power, this reminds us of Lord Acton's maxim that "power corrupts and absolute power corrupts absolutely." Certainly, the gentlemen who framed our constitution were cognizant of the ill effects of the centralization of power.

However, in any hierarchical system where efficiency is a necessary condition, the allocation of power is inherent in the need to explicitly define responsibility and authority. The management of power is perhaps the greatest challenge to the organizational executive. Executives who comprehend the nature, extent and limitations of their power are those who most wisely guide their organizations without being seduced into the trap of egotism. Conversely, evidence suggests that some of those who use power most unwisely are those persons who deny its existence or that they hold power.

Becoming a senior manager, especially a CEO, is making a career change. The job requires:

— a high level of understanding of the context the organization functions within

— an ability to comprehend how every decision cascades throughout an organization and will have both positive and negative consequences

— an awareness of the law of unintended consequences

— a keen perception of who the key stakeholders are, what each values and will fight to preserve

This understanding then needs to be coupled with an ability to use both formal and informal power.

The central difference between wisdom and executive wisdom is that executive wisdom comes with considerable power.

Many of the executives I have worked with are able to comprehend and balance the complexities within organizational systems. One of the tools they often use is some version of the Franklin Table, or what some people appropriately call the Power Table. Benjamin Franklin, in *Poor Richard's Almanack*, suggested decision making is enhanced by following this simple procedure. First, he suggested writing down the decision. Moving from the spoken to the written word increases rigorousness of thought, clarifies the decision and makes it easier to communicate. Franklin then suggested drawing a vertical line down the center of the paper, creating two columns, and listing the pros and cons, opportunities and threats, benefits and costs etc. Considering all the possible variables facilitates a more exhaustive analysis of the decision. It is also effective to invite the input of knowledgeable others into the process. The power of this tool is that it forces executives, particularly if they invite others into the process, to examine every knowable facet of the decision.

Following up on the Franklin analysis, it is often valuable to develop distinct pictures of the very best and the very worst outcomes. Although we can rarely do this with much accuracy, it markedly reduces the level of uncertainty, helps us to conceptualize what the range of outcomes may be and begin to think about how to respond to these possible results.

Finally, because we must always remind ourselves that most decisions are heavily influenced by emotions, we need to thoroughly examine our motives for the decision. I am fond of recommending to managers "that they sleep on it" as part of the process of making an important decision. This usually changes the emotional context, contributes to more reasonable judgments and thus better decisions. Most effective executives appreciate that the "feel" of a decision is an integral aspect of the process. Perhaps we need to develop tools to more formally integrate this element into our decision making.

Although it is probably not possible to teach wisdom in any formal manner, it is possible for executives to use tools that help them integrate a broader consideration of the situation into their decision making.

Go To:
Leadership Is an Important Organizational
Performance Driver (3.1)
Principles vs. Rules (2.7)
Tactical to Strategic (2.8)

3.19

Never Waste a Good Crisis

Managers in organizations initially see a crisis as a threat, but by mentally re-framing it, they can perceive it as an opportunity. The Chinese have a pair of ideograms that mean "opportunity in crisis" and connote the conditions under which change is likely to occur, and the conditions whereby some opportune moments distinguish themselves from the countless undistinguished moments of history. Over some time, I have observed that dramatic action by government only seems to happen when there is serious and widely accepted and agreed-upon crisis.

The leadership literature also shows us that an element in the development of leadership is a personal crucible. The second definition of crucible is a set of circumstances where people are subjected to forces that test them and often make them change.

It is interesting that recent thinking and writing on leadership indicates that leaders are formed by such events in their lives. How we mentally frame the event, as in "it's the end of the world" vs. "where is the silver lining," generally determines if we will emerge from such a crisis better or worse. I am convinced that nothing, especially people, remains the same. Events force improvement or deterioration in our lives. If we do nothing we decline; if we take the initiative, we usually improve. So each of us can examine crises in the context of our lives and look for the positive change that we can make of it.

It is a truism in organizations that leaders should never waste a good crisis.

Taking initiative is an American characteristic that is deeply embedded in the ethic that as individuals we take personal responsibility to make things better. Recently, I heard a story about a business that suffered a catastrophic event. Customers committed to the survival of the business came in and ordered products. They then prepaid, telling the business owner to deliver the products when she was able. We often see such examples of altruism in crises.

It is a truism in organizations that leaders should never waste a good crisis. A crisis is an opportunity to make a wide range of changes very rapidly without encountering resistance because there is a larger issue driving events. It is also an opportunity for people in key positions to demonstrate that collaborative actions have the greatest benefit and to show the organization the breadth and depth of their leadership excellence. Their leadership will energize others throughout the organization to pitch in and help out. My own experience has led me to conclude that people are generally at their very best when things are at their worst.

The management literature is now showing evidence of a demonstrated side effect of collaboration. A key element to any competitive organization regardless of the sector (for profit, nonprofit or public) is innovation. Innovation mostly happens when people with disparate expertise come together to solve a pressing problem.

I once consulted with a turn-around manager who was given the charge by corporate to enter a deeply troubled manufacturing plant and fix it or close it. He chose to begin with a general meeting of all the people in the plant and invited them to work with him and the management team to make the changes necessary in quality and productivity to assure the continued operation of the facility. I was deeply moved by the manner in which he cast this crisis not as a threat — shape up or you're toast — but as an opportunity to fundamentally change the functioning of the organization. Needless to say, the level of communication, cooperation and collaboration was impressive.

What can we conclude from the evidence on crises and crucibles about the change process? That in situations where there is an over-arching crisis, an effective leader can mobilize people and make change. Lesson learned.

Go To:
The Power of Information (2.3)
Engagement and Decision Making (2.5)
Courage: Managers into Leaders (2.9)

3.20

Harness the Power of Mentoring in Your Business

As we have moved from an economy that is muscle-based to one that is mind-driven, the development of high-performance people becomes more critical to the success of the organization. Much has been written about mentoring and coaching as tools that may be better suited to the needs of the information-driven organization.

Consider this example. Many companies are assigning "buddies" to new hires. They pair newbies with capable, experienced employees who have shown that they are good at helping others rapidly develop new skills. This has been shown to be an effective tool for socializing new employees. It is particularly valuable where workplace safety is a serious concern. So, is a buddy a coach or a mentor? Both roles are probably enacted in this situation, but the dominant one is likely to be showing the new employee how to do something and then providing feedback and encouragement to rapidly improve performance.

A mentor is someone, usually older and more experienced, who provides advice and support to and watches over and fosters the progress of

> **A mentor is someone, usually older and more experienced, who provides advice and support to and watches over and fosters the progress of a younger, less-experienced person.**

a younger, less-experienced person.

Consider this example of mentoring. An executive selects a high-potential person to serve as her assistant for perhaps one year. Here are the primary opportunities the executive provides for the assistant: First, the executive introduces the assistant to many influential people within and without the organization who have a significant impact on the business. This is an important networking experience for the assistant.

Second, the executive takes the assistant to all of her meetings. The mentoring goes something like this. As they proceed to the meeting, the executive briefs the assistant on who is going to be there, what the purpose of the meeting is and shares an overview of her strategy for accomplishing the agenda. After the meeting, the executive debriefs the assistant with questions such as: What is your impression of each of the participants? How did you think the meeting went? Did you understand why I did not enact the strategy that I outlined as we went to the meeting? This usually leads to a discussion about the dynamics of the organization that is invaluable to the assistant and helps the executive be more reflective.

Third, the assistant essentially becomes the executive's shadow, following her throughout the day, even to one-on-one meetings covering confidential topics. The executive is role-modeling her behavior for the assistant. This is a powerful experience because it gives the assistant an intimate knowledge of how an executive functions.

Fourth, the executive assigns readings and each week she and the assistant discuss these in-depth. The readings may be key internal documents representing important aspects of each of the key operations of the organization, more general information about the business or about current management practices. Two general sources of information often used in a situation such as this are *The Wall Street Journal* and the *Harvard*

Business Review.

You can immediately comprehend that this is a very intense relationship that can result in orders of magnitude of improvement in the assistant's understanding of the organization and the role, responsibilities and day-to-day behavior of the executive. It is also very expensive because it requires an executive who has a unique and highly developed skill set and makes a huge investment of her time. This means the selection procedure for this process is critical because the organization must identify a person who will profit from this investment, who has a well-developed set of cognitive and emotional skills and who is utterly trustworthy because the potential for serious mischief is immense.

Mentoring, where these conditions pertain, works because it is a powerful process for imbuing the assistant with enormous amounts of tacit knowledge.

Go To:
Improving Your Communications through Active Listening (1.3)
Coaching to Improve Performance (1.6)
The Information Continuum (3.15)

Organizations Come in Three Varieties

Those of you who are old enough to have had the dubious honor of taking Latin in high school will recall that Julius Caesar began his Commentaries by observing that, "All Gaul is divided into three parts."

So also does the universe of organizations exist in three flavors: private for-profit, private nonprofit and public. Without exception, all organizations fall into one of these categories, although there is some blending. Typically, people spend most of their work-lives in one of these sectors. Understanding and appreciating the nature of the three sectors and how they complement each other — and provide the foundation for a vibrant economy and a sound democracy — is useful knowledge for any informed citizen. Let's elucidate by examining each against a common set of characteristics: their purpose, ownership, funding, organizational structure, law and strengths/weaknesses.

The purpose of the public sector is inscribed on the sides of police vehicles in many communities: to protect and to serve. Government exists to "establish justice, insure domestic tranquility, provide for the common defense, promote the general welfare and secure the blessings of liberty."

The public sector is owned by the people, particularly those of us who exercise our franchise. It draws its operating monies from the use of many different forms of taxation. It exists within the constraints of public sector law, which generally means that elected officials and rule-writers define the boundaries of its functioning. As such, the public sector is usually bureaucratic in its organizational structure.

This mix of three sectors provides a striking and effective use of organizational purpose and resources.

Here in the Midwest, we have very good government at all levels and it works well to provide the basic infrastructure and services we need to live our lives. The public sector also often offers the first step in employment for those who are climbing from the bottom of the socio-economic ladder, and its employees have a measure of employment security that does not exist in other sectors. It is however, very political, rule-driven and resistant to change. Fortunately in the United States, we have a public sector that can change rapidly in response to crises as is amply demonstrated by perusal of our history.

The private for-profit sector exists to create wealth. It does this by offering people an enormous range of opportunities to begin and operate their own businesses and it then distributes this wealth by creating jobs. Businesses are funded by the sales of products and services, and more recently, by the sale of information. About 70 percent of businesses are owned by individuals or families.

American law offers many mechanisms to form profit-making companies: closely held and publicly traded corporations, partnerships, sole proprietors, etc. This variety of structures permits a wide breadth of possible strategies for entrepreneurs and business people. This means that a private sector employer can treat her/his employees much better or much worse than in the public sector.

One of the great strengths of the private sector is its immense ability to leverage ideas and monies to create new wealth. In addition, the intense level of competition can spur innovation and creativity. Throughout our historical trajectory, with a few notable exceptions, our for-profit sector has steadily improved the financial well being of citizens and immigrants.

One of the unique contributions of America to the concept of organizations is the third sector: The private nonprofit organization. Nonprofit companies exist to do good. A number of concerned individuals can come together and create an organization that is designed explicitly to help others. Such an organization is owned by an unpaid board of trustees and often derives all of its funding from charitable contributions, but some also receive monies from the government.

Nonprofits come in a wide variety of types and sizes, from local centers for the mentally ill, disabled people and senior citizens, to large multi-billion dollar organizations such as the Bill and Melinda Gates Foundation. Because these organizations operate with neither the pressures of profitability nor the limitations of politics, they are often able to make extraordinary contributions to our society.

Knowledgeable ex-pat business people who have spent several years in the U.S. often comment to me about how this mix of three sectors provides a striking and effective use of organizational purpose and resources. Having had the opportunity to work in and consult with all three types of organizations I am quick to agree and to appreciate how this triad makes it possible to balance needs and resources in an appropriate and effective fashion that many other cultures lack.

Go To:
Organizations and Management (2.1)
Leadership Is an Important Organizational
Performance Driver (3.1)
Executive Wisdom: Context (3.14)

Understanding and Using Consulting as a Competitive Advantage

Recent studies on the growth of occupations show that one of the fastest-growing careers is consulting. This is a reflection of the changing nature of our economy. We used to hear about how we were moving from an industrial economy where the typical worker is a laborer to a service economy where the typical worker is a clerk. Now it is pretty clear that we have moved solidly into an information economy.

In 1988, Peter Drucker suggested that this was happening and that the typical worker in an information economy is a knowledge worker. Richard Florida more recently recast this definition somewhat and coined the term "creative worker." The important point is that first-world economies are being driven by the rapid flow of information and the tool of choice to manage these elements is technology.

Understanding the exponential explosion of knowledge in recent decades, it is easy to see why consulting has grown proportionally. Simply put, the corpus of current knowledge in every field is so vast that even a large company cannot hire enough people to "know everything." Therefore, most productive organizations decide what their core business is and staff to maximize the knowledge base of their core functions. They then engage consultants for their expertise as needed. This trend has resulted in outsourcing, hiring outside companies to carry out functions that are not part of the core business. Perhaps the best-known area where this happens is in IT. Companies such as IBM have completely redesigned their business model to compete in this market.

Today, the leaders of even small companies need to understand how they can leverage the mostly tacit knowledge of consultants to improve their productivity. Understanding the nature of consulting can help you use this resource.

Consulting might be thought of as coming in two flavors: task and process. Actually, consultants operate everywhere along this dimension. Most consulting is a mixture of task and process. Consider IT as an example. IT consultants not only can assist you with what software and hardware you need, but can help you discover how to derive maximum advantage from the systems as well as train your people in the effective use of these systems. In many respects, consulting reflects the increased emphasis being placed on the **how** as well as the **what** of business functions.

The types of consulting that can produce the greatest productivity gains are those focused on the development of a company's people, particularly managers and leaders, and the organizational matrix they function within. Most of us who have managed in or consulted to organizations appreciate how difficult behavior change can be to accomplish. A distinguished psychologist wrote, "Habits are cobwebs that grow into cables." We are all creatures of habit who prefer to live in environments that we control and that are predictable. For organizations to change and become more productive, people must change their behavior, and this is a challenge even for the very motivated. Perhaps the most salient example of human inertia is how little behavior change results from traditional training programs requiring interpersonal skills change such as sales, management, customer service or leadership.

The most critical step in developing a relationship with a consultant is engaging one who works well with you.

Today, particularly in America, we are seeing the rapid development of consulting organizations that are focused on helping organizational leaders get greater productivity from their people. Understanding the consulting process and how to work effectively with a consultant can be a competitive advantage for organizations of any size.

The most critical step in developing a relationship with a consultant is engaging one who works well with you. The starting point is to tap into your professional network and ask colleagues you trust. Many consultants get most of their work through referrals from satisfied clients. Set up a meeting with this person and develop an understanding of their services, keeping in mind the task-process dimension, as well as your comfort level with this person. Remember, you are letting this person inside your organization and trust is a key element of the process. Get off to a good start by explicitly defining who the client is, the level of confidentiality, sharing expectations and developing a workplan that includes what, when, who and how much.

For consultant and client, a productive working relationship can be remarkable. At the most basic level, it yields an ongoing conversation about the organization, its people and reflections on management and leadership. This is a dialogue that both parties can actively participate in, learn from and use to improve performance.

Go To:
Leadership is an Important Organizational
Performance Driver (3.1)
What are the Characteristics of a Great Workplace? (4.6)
If You See a Bathroom, Use It! (5.2)

3.23

How 'Nice' Managers
Unknowingly Cause Havoc

When we hear reports of bad management, they usually involve examples of the controlling, authoritarian, emotionally abusive type of manager. Perhaps this is the case because such persons are easily identified by their inappropriate behavior. There is, however, another type of manager that has equally negative effects on the performance and emotional state of his employees. Surprisingly, the best description of this person is "the nice guy," or perhaps more accurately, "the too-nice guy."

Most of the core characteristics of managers rest on easily understood dimensions. One that we are most familiar with is the task-relationship dimension. In this, the challenge is to balance task (getting the work done) with relationship (nurturing effective interpersonal relationships). As in most systems of this type, the best performers are those who manage a reasonable balance between the extremes and don't fall into the trap of operating at one end of the continuum to the exclusion of the other.

Clearly, the earlier-described manager cares not a whit about how people feel as long as the work gets done to his satisfaction. But what is the result from a style of management practice that over-emphasizes relationships?

When people become managers, they have to consider their personal styles and their assumptions about the nature of work and of people. It is reasonable to think of the first promotion to a management position as a career change. This can be a very difficult transition depending on the basic nature of the competency that resulted in the promotion and the person's ability to comprehend what management practice is and how to enact this new role.

Consider the example of a nurse who is promoted to a manager position. This person made a career choice to become a nurse, engaged in considerable education to build a knowledge base and then successfully practiced this career, probably with great personal satisfaction, for many years. Then one day, probably because of her competence and interpersonal style as a nurse, she was promoted. This is a dramatic change in her social role. She has jumped from what is essentially a helping profession where it is easy to be the good guy, to a profession where many decisions she makes will result in less-than-pleasant responses from others.

She also has to dramatically change her relationships with her direct reports, especially if she is managing what used to be her co-workers. She probably hasn't had much training in management and may not have a mentor. It's easy to see the problems that may result. Too often in this situation, the new manager chooses to either become very authoritarian or tilts to the opposite extreme and tries to become everyone's friend. Both strategies produce poor results.

Recently, I worked with a vice president who chose the latter strategy sometime in his early development as a manager. After working with him for an extended time, I began to understand why he was having problems with his peers, his direct reports and why his department was not functioning very well. He was the ultimate people pleaser and made an outstanding first impression. He appeared to listen, interacted appropriately and seemed well anchored in a participative style of management. I could not understand why his boss reported that many key people in the organization did not trust him and often stated that his practice with them was to "spin." Strategy and coaching sessions were always agreeable and explicit goals usually resulted.

His management style was dramatically illustrated by a situation with one of his non-performing managers. This direct report was charging around the organization doing what he pleased and causing many problems, usually involving how he treated people. I have seen quite a few of this type and they usually respond well to a firm, direct, demanding management style. So, the VP and I set out to work with this person. My core advice to the VP was something like, "This guy owes you a lot, you have a very good personal relationship with him and you must demand that he change while promising as much assistance as he needs." After several weeks, no apparent change was visible and the manager in question had become more troubled.

When people become managers, they have to consider their personal styles and their assumptions about the nature of work and of people.

After some investigation, I realized that the VP was a "too-nice guy." The too-nice guy typically has a couple powerful needs that overwhelm his ability to effectively manage: He wants people to like him and he doesn't want there to be any conflict in his workspace. This means in many situations he makes promises to people, to immediately please, that he probably will not carry through. The effect on his peers is that he often doesn't deliver and they begin to mistrust him.

He also has difficulty giving negative feedback to non-performing direct reports. Most people go ahead and do their jobs, but for some this lack of direction is a recipe for disaster. A troubled employee may adopt a behavioral strategy that is self-defeating and will receive zero feedback, so he cannot readjust the behavior. In addition, morale in the area will deteriorate because initiatives are sometimes not carried to completion for any reason that employees can understand.

Usually in organizations, problems result in actions that produce improvements. A manager with a too-nice style misses these opportunities because he is too conflict-avoidant to identify and address the issues. The unit itself can drift out of control because people lack a shared sense of direction. Ergo: chaos. It seems that for this type of manager it is more important to be liked than to be respected.

The most disturbing aspect of this situation is that the too-nice manager's say/do ratio deteriorates. This can lead to ethical issues. It is a reasonable ethical expectation in any organization that a manager not allow an employee to fail. In the above example, without direct feedback, clear expectations and assertive ongoing coaching, the direct report will fail.

Interestingly, this type of manager is more difficult to help change than the authoritarian described above. For reasons that are unclear, it is easier to "dial back" an aggressive person than to "dial up" a weak one.

Go To:
Candor Is a Valuable Trait in Successful Leaders (1.5)
Action-Oriented Style (2.6)
Courage: Managers into Leaders (2.9)

Unit 4:
Motivation and Morale, Jobs and Job Loss

Understanding the complexity of human motivation is essential to understanding how to lead and manage people. It is also central to understanding and enhancing our personal and professional performance. Therefore, this unit complements the management practices, leadership and personal-development units. The first six segments discuss the many dimensions of motivation and present an overview of human motivation as well and deepening our understanding of how critical emotion is in the formation and maintenance of job satisfaction. The segments also include concrete, actionable actions to manage our own and others' motivation.

1. A Multi-Dimensional View of Motivation and Morale
2. What Is Your Attitude Toward Work?
3. What's Your Proper Fit in the Workplace?
4. How Are Your Relationships in the Workplace?
5. What Are Your Motivators and Demotivators?
6. What Are the Characteristics of a Great Workplace?

The second set of segments is distinct from the motivation materials. They are important to understand if you are interested in improving productivity in the workplace. This material fits particularly well with the segment in Unit 1, "Driving quality improvements with the internal customer model." The first two of these segments review the job as a social contract and the third examines the job as a social role. If you believe that the building block of cultures is families, then the building block of companies is jobs. The careful development of good job fit can do much to improve organizational performance.

7. Understanding the Job as a Social Contract
8. Skills Needed for the Job Can Change Employment Landscape
9. Aid Understanding by Defining the Job as a Social Role

The third set on job loss is more personal. If you have lost your job, or have a friend or colleague who has been separated from an organization for whatever reason, these segments can help that person to place such a difficult experience in context.

10. So, You Just Lost Your Job! Now What?
11. How to Find a Job After Being Fired
12. Finding a New Job is a Group Effort

A Multi-Dimensional View of Motivation and Morale

Morale, motivation and employee satisfaction: What are they and what drives them? Because this topic is so complex, I hardly know where to begin.

Human motivation is at least as complex as the weather, and we can barely forecast that the day after tomorrow. What is needed is a model to give any such discussion structure.

With apologies to psychologists (not really), here is what your professor didn't tell you in Psychology 101. All human behavior comes in three flavors: We are creatures of thought (cognition), feeling (emotion) and action (behavior). After this, it gets really hard (like the weather. But we love to talk about it like the weather and after all, what is gossip but our personal analyses of other people?). Think of a triangle with these components at each corner. These components interact with and influence the others continuously.

Much of our behavior is driven by thought; we decide to do something and we do it. This voluntary (thought-driven) type of behavior is called operant because it operates on the environment. Similarly, by thinking and imagining sad or happy events we can elicit negative or positive emotional reactions.

Emotional behavior is called respondent because it is largely driven by stimuli, some of which we can manage ourselves, but many of which are essentially involuntary. Learning to manage our emotional behavior is a major life-long developmental challenge for human beings.

Some of our behavior is driven by emotion, and the more powerful and negative the emotion, the more effect it has on us. Consider how powerful emotion is in locking down vivid memories. Who cannot remember the personal where, what and how of the situation they were in when they heard, or in some cases saw the Twin Towers fall, or the moment we learned that a parent or dear friend had died?

Some emotions also elicit powerful protective behaviors. In a high-threat situation, the impulse is to fight or flee. Controlling these seemingly hard-wired emotional responses is difficult. Consider the number of people in our worlds that we describe as impulsive.

Many people underestimate the power of emotion in human beings. Emotion not only energizes people, but can heavily influence actions in a fashion that is often unreasonable and can be irrational. I have a respected colleague who notes "stress makes people stupid." If you understand that stress is a modern and softer synonym for negative emotions, particularly fear, this is quite obvious. Most of the really poor decisions that we make in our lives were made thoughtlessly under conditions of high emotion. Effective decision making is of course a form of thought.

I have a respected colleague who notes 'stress makes people stupid.'

Finally, our actions and those of others affect our feelings and thoughts. For almost all of us, except those who are sociopaths, treating people kindly and respectfully makes us feel good about ourselves. The converse is also the case.

One of the major ways we learn new skills and knowledge is by doing. You can read very deeply about how to work on a personal computer, but the only way to really learn, for most of us, is to sit at the computer and let it become a teaching machine.

Morale or satisfaction is a complex combination of thoughts and feelings that energize or de-energize our behavior (actions) in the workplace (and elsewhere). This definition is also close to the definition of attitude.

Go To:
Respectful Behavior (2.4)
What Is Your Attitude Toward Work? (4.2)
Self-Talk to Success or Failure? (5.4)

What Is Your Attitude Toward Work?

Imagine that we could take a brief walk through the Middle Ages (with apologies to *Fortune* magazine, where I read this story), a time when life was hard, brutal and short.

We first encounter a young man who is working on a large stone with a mallet and chisel. He is sweating, swearing and is clearly very unhappy. "What are you doing we ask?" He shouts at us, "I am cutting this stone and it is damn hard work!"

Continuing on, we encounter another young man working on a stone. He is more relaxed and the quality of the stonework seems better to us. We ask, "What are you doing?" He answers, "I am shaping a stone for a building." Finally we come to a third young man. He is whistling and upbeat, the chips are flying, the stone looks nearly perfect. We ask, "What are you doing?" He pauses for a moment and then answers, "I am building a cathedral!" Are you toiling on a difficult stone or building a cathedral? The choice is yours.

This is a story about attitudes, and such stories are often more subtle than this one appears. It is clear that some people bring an "attitude" to the workplace, which means they are not pleasant to be around most of the time. In the past years, many companies have realized the importance of attitudes and some now hire for attitude on the belief that it is easier to train people with a good attitude than to try to change the attitudes of difficult people.

Attitudes are probably not hard-wired, but they are certainly shaped by our interactions with our environment. Warren Bennis, who writes lucidly about leadership, has noted that leaders are shaped by powerful and difficult events in their lives. Our ability to find meaning in negative events and to emerge from these events stronger is a predictor of leadership and of successful living in general. For some people, the opposite seems to be the case. They emerge from adversity bitter, cynical and untrusting.

Returning to the three-part model of human behavior that we covered in the previous segment (thoughts, feelings and actions), can we use our strengths to reshape our attitudes toward situations such as work? A person with a negative attitude must start with the understanding, at a feeling level, that this view of the world is having a negative effect on the quality of his life. The strategy is to then use thoughts and actions to change the feelings that motivate the bad attitudes.

It is necessary for the person to use the greatest ally in change, the mind, to begin to reframe how they perceive the world and what they expect from people. They can do this by talking to themselves in a more positive manner, stopping their negative thoughts, reasoning with themselves and trying to see the other person's perspective. These are all mental strategies that help people reframe their internal perceptions of the world.

Attitudes are probably not hard-wired, but they are certainly shaped by our interactions with our environment.

The other strategy is to begin to use new behaviors that invite people to change their response behavior in a more positive way. These include simple courtesies such as saying thank you and please, not voicing negative opinions, using thoughtful and kind comments, asking questions and really listening to the answers. All these are behaviors that the person with an "attitude" almost never uses.

Basically, what I am suggesting is taking control of your life by changing your innermost thoughts and your overt behavior. This will begin to change the feelings that motivate the bad attitudes. If you believe as I do that human behavior is highly reciprocal — what you give is what you get — these changes are likely to have a marked effect on the quality of your interactions with the world in general and the workplace in particular.

However, there are some difficulties with this strategy. First, because negative emotions are more powerful than positive, one misstep back to the old behaviors will substantially set the process back. Multiple missteps will pretty much convince everyone that the whole effort is a ruse and greatly reduce the likelihood of success.

Second, it takes a long time before people begin to believe that this is the new you and stop waiting for the old behaviors to appear. A poor manager with an attitude may find, when he changes, that it will take some of his coworkers a couple of years to begin to trust the new person. For this reason, it might be better to make a fresh start in a new workplace, but that's going to be a problem if your "attitude" persists.

Go To:
Respectful Behavior (2.4)
A Multi-Dimensional View of Motivation and Morale (4.1)
If You See a Bathroom, Use It! (5.2)

4.3

What's Your Proper Fit in the Workplace?

Probably the best predictor of morale and satisfaction in the workplace is having a job you do well and enjoy doing.

If we build cultures with families, then we build companies with jobs. One of the most remarkable aspects of the American economy is the sheer number and variety of jobs. And if you don't like any of the more than 145 million jobs out there, you can easily create your own by starting a business.

For most Americans, their job defines who they are; ask people who they are and they tell you what they do. You can learn more about people by asking them about the families they grew up in and the jobs they work in than any other possible inquiries. Jobs bring people an income, an identity and a social-support system. Good jobs are the major source of social mobility in this country.

I occasionally work with someone who becomes very upset on Sunday night or Monday morning when they realize they must return to an extremely unsatisfying job. Likewise, most of the mature, well-adjusted adults I know have personally satisfying jobs. What accounts for this too-often dramatic difference?

Living and working successfully is like playing poker. Your parents and the environment deal you a hand. How you play the hand is the key to job satisfaction. To play your hand strategically, you must know what cards you hold; so it is with work-life.

Probably the best predictor of morale and satisfaction in the workplace is having a job you do well and enjoy doing.

Understanding who we are and what our strengths and weaknesses are has been called intra-personal intelligence. Our ability to understand ourselves is called insight, looking into ourselves. Socrates, an ancient Greek philosopher who had a bad experience with hemlock, said, "Know thyself." More recently, Peter Drucker wrote an extraordinarily powerful article titled "Managing Oneself." I have read this article dozens of times, and it never fails to energize my ongoing quest to better understand myself. Puzzle out what your strengths are and then find a job that maximizes your strengths and minimizes your weaknesses.

There is a movement afoot in the behavioral sciences called "Positive Psychology." It comes from the simultaneous insight of a number of leaders of that art that too much time has been spent on the study of dysfunctional people. Why not, they rightly inquire, study the behavior of high-performance people and help others to adopt these high-performance practices?

One of the foremost proponents of this approach was a fine gentleman named Don Clifton, who until his untimely death was the leader of the Gallup Corp. With his leadership, Gallup has been collecting data from the workplace that begins to elucidate the problem of how we can enhance our day-to-day performance at work. One of the products of this work is an online assessment tool called the StrengthsFinder, which is accompanied by a book titled *StrengthsFinder 2.0*. By going online to a Gallup web site, it is possible to assess your five major strengths and then begin to develop personal strategies to enhance your strengths. This tool is easy to use with yourself and others because instead of focusing on your weaknesses it defines your strengths. At the suggestion of a client, I used the tool and was delighted at its findings. It helped me understand how I have created a job for myself that plays to my strengths, not my weaknesses.

Aside from the barrier of not being willing to understand our strengths and weaknesses, lacking insight, the second great barrier to finding the perfect job is the myth of the "well-rounded person." It is a widely accepted piece of tacit knowledge that effective people and effective organizations do a few things well. This insight comes from the understanding that we live in a complex world that is becoming increasingly more complex every day. During the Renaissance it was possible to be a Renaissance man, but today the world and work are too complex to us to know everything. Over my years of consulting with leaders and managers in companies, I have noticed that the best of them are "sharp as a tack," not "well-rounded."

Our ability to define and hold a job that fits us is a lifelong quest. We change and the jobs we work in change and the companies those jobs are in change. Thus, the challenge is to continuously assess our fit and readjust our careers to maintain and enhance our satisfaction.

Go To:
Understanding the Job as a Social Contract (4.7)
Skills Needed for the Job Can Change Employment Landscape (4.8)
Aid Understanding by Defining the Job as a Social Role (4.9)

How Are Your Relationships in the Workplace?

In this series about morale, we have thus far examined the complexity of morale and satisfaction, the attitudes we bring to work and how well we fit in our jobs. What about the quality of the relationships we have in the workplace?

Several years ago, the Gallup Corp. developed an employee satisfaction tool they call the Q12. Based on more than 8 million cases in thousands of companies they have used statistical analyses to discover the 12 best questions to measure employee satisfaction. This is part of the assessment that *Fortune* magazine uses for the "Best Places to Work" issue.

Perhaps the most curious finding of these studies was that the single best predictor of employee satisfaction was the response to the question "I have a best friend at work." People who responded favorably to this query tended to have much higher job satisfaction than those who did not. The researchers at Gallup were surprised at this result because at first blush it appears that who people choose as friends is not something that can be managed.

I once heard a very thoughtful person state that we can measure the quality of our lives by the quality of our relationships. Clearly, work is no longer a solitary endeavor — no more monks hand-copying ancient texts — but occurs through our interactions with people. These people may be customers, bosses, vendors, consultants or co-workers, and with each of these, we have the ability to enhance or degrade the relationship.

Following up on the Q12 finding, Gallup has published a fascinating book titled *"Vital Friends: The People You Can't Afford To Live Without."* Tom Rath, the author, begins the book with a chapter discussing the importance and power of our friends' expectations for us. He shares a dramatic example of a person who essentially lost all of his friends and with them the expectations that made him a successful person. He declined to become a street person and rose from the street because one person "expected him to be somebody" and communicated this expectation through a vibrant relationship. The book continues to build on the theme of the power of relationships to enhance our lives and, naturally, because it is Gallup, takes us to an online tool to assess the quality

'I never met a man I didn't like.'
- WILL ROGERS

and types of our relationships. This is an easy and intriguing read. I recommend it as a tool to reframe how you look at your relationships.

Perhaps the most important relationship in the workplace, if not the best predictor of satisfaction, is with your immediate boss. A good boss can help you succeed; a bad boss can make you fail regardless of how hard you try. Rather than writing a paragraph, let me share two lists that I have acquired of peoples' perceptions in the workplace.

Here are the behaviors of the "boss from hell:" sarcasm, not listening and ignoring, sniping, punishing all for one, breaking confidence, asking for input when the decision has been made, asking for input on trivial decisions, not explaining why, writing a policy to solve a problem and coming to meetings late.

In contrast, here is employees' "wish list" for a great boss: asks for and values my opinion, listens to my suggestions, takes my ideas seriously, checks with me before making a decision that affects my work, would defend me in a meeting of supervisors, explains goals clearly, gives me latitude in deciding how to carry out a project, saves criticism for one-on-one, gives lots of feedback, comes to meetings on time and runs good meetings.

It is easy to see that good bosses care about people and treat people with respect. I am often bewildered at how hard these simple courtesies seem to be for some people.

An important skill with regard to your boss is learning how to manage her. In an article titled "Managing Your Boss" in the *Harvard Business Review*, John Gabarro and John Kotter note that forging ties with your boss based on understanding and mutual respect will result in both of you being more effective. What they are saying is that you should take responsibility for managing the relationship with your boss.

Go To:
To Improve Productivity, Try Saying Thank You (1.7)
Respectful Behavior (2.4)
Improving Your Personal and Professional Productivity (5.1)

4.5

What Are Your Motivators and Demotivators?

In this series of segments about morale in the workplace, we have examined the complexity of morale and satisfaction, the attitudes we bring to work, how well we fit in our jobs and our relationships at work. What about the very basic aspects of the workplace that de-motivate and motivate people?

It's impossible to review this area without paying homage to Fredrick Herzberg's classic article from the *Harvard Business Review*, "One More Time: How Do You Motivate Employees?" This article is probably the most thoughtful discussion of motivation that has been written in the past three decades, and is widely cited and reprinted.

Mr. Herzberg begins by defining the most basic, and poorest form, of motivation in the workplace: KITA. Kick in the Ass is the most simple-minded and perhaps the most often used form of motivation. It is essentially based on one emotion: fear; fear of losing one's job, fear of verbal or emotional abuse, fear of ridicule, fear of... on and on and on.

We can all imagine plenty of things to be fearful of in the workplace. My summer job during college was in a lead smelter in western Montana. It was a dirty, tough and dangerous working environment where the foremen basically managed by threatening people. What did I learn from that? That I never want to work in such an environment.

That's fine for a college graduate, but some people do not have a choice. What must that be like? Research shows that fear as a motivator produces two kinds of behavior in people: escape and avoidance. In an environment where we need peoples' participation, their skills and their knowledge, do we really want to motivate them to escape or avoid?

Mr. Herzberg makes a compelling case for what he considers to be the two overriding factors that contribute to motivation in very different ways. He notes that the factors that produce job satisfaction are separate and distinct from those that produce job dissatisfaction, and that job satisfaction is not simply the absence of job dissatisfaction.

The dissatisfaction factors are related to KITA, and he refers to them as hygiene factors. These factors get you to a neutral environment when they are met but do not motivate superior performance. These factors are: company policy and administration, supervision, working conditions, salary, status and security. When these conditions are absent, they produce high levels of job dissatisfaction. Without some basic level of these conditions, it is very difficult to build an environment that motivates high levels of performance.

We can conclude that there are as many possible combinations of work that produce job satisfaction or dissatisfaction as there are people.

The motivators are achievement, recognition, the work itself, responsibility, advancement and the opportunity for personal growth. All of these are often referred to as intrinsic because they work only when the person has an intrinsic need to satisfy these basic psychological needs.

This is where motivation becomes complex and confusing. Although most people are motivated by such conditions as responsibility and recognition, some are not. In fact, some are de-motivated by such conditions. Likewise, for a small but significant proportion of people, such variables as security, status or company policy are sufficient motivators to produce levels of job satisfaction that are adequate for them. I noted when I started this series that human behavior is much more complex than the weather. So much for an easily understood set of facts that gives us a simple strategy for motivating people.

By now you are thinking, "Why is there such a perception of compensation as a motivator?" Clearly, Mr. Herzberg puts compensation into the hygiene factor. This means that everyone has some particular level of compensation that is satisfactory, and once they reach it let the coasting begin. This is but one example of a multitude of possible scenarios of employee motivation.

The challenge for the manager is to identify this hygiene situation when it happens and to tailor the motivational system to the elements that produce extreme job satisfaction. Sometimes this is very difficult, perhaps impossible, given the constraints of the typical workplace. The challenge to each person who wants to work in a highly motivating environment is to identify the most important hygiene factors and motivators and then find a work setting that plays to those elements. In short, what we can conclude from this discussion is that there are as many possible combinations of work that produce job satisfaction or dissatisfaction as there are people.

Go To:
What Are the Characteristics of a Great Workplace? (4.6)
Understanding the Job as a Social Contract (4.7)
Aid Understanding by Defining the Job as a Social Role (4.9)

What Are the Characteristics of a Great Workplace?

Thus far in this series of segments about morale, we have presented a model to explain peoples' behavior at work, the attitudes we bring to work, how well we fit in our jobs, our relationships at work and a usable model of motivation. What about the very nature of the company we work for?

You can learn a lot from peoples' response to the question, "Where do you work?" At one extreme, people try to duck the question or provide an ambiguous answer that discourages further inquiry or occasionally launch a long monologue about how badly their employer treats them. At the other extreme, people begin to tell you how great it is to work at XYZ. Clearly, how people think and feel about their company has an effect on their motivation and morale.

It is generally the case that people want to work for a company they are proud to acknowledge as their employer. What are the core characteristics of such a company?

The most powerful variable driving organizational performance is leadership. As I have noted in one of the previous articles on leadership, there are many different styles of leadership. All of these diverse leaders drive a culture that has some common aspects.

These leaders model and demand the highest ethical behavior from their people. Ethical behavior is the standard and the definition of ethical behavior, both internally and externally, is explicit and practiced by all. Violations of the ethical code are dealt with thoughtfully and swiftly, particularly when the offender is part of the managerial structure.

It is generally the case that people want to work for a company they are proud to acknowledge as their employer.

The leader of such a company spends much of his/her time on managing communications within and without the organization. Their philosophy about communication could be summarized as, "The better informed people are the better they perform." Peter Drucker said, "Information is data endowed with relevance and purpose." Communication is the systematic management of information and every manager is expected to communicate and over-communicate with people throughout the company.

The leader uses the power of the position to set the standard for communication very high. No "mushroom management" around here.

Another characteristic of the leader is to develop a system that optimizes decision making by making the decision as close as possible to the work. This practice invites peoples' input where appropriate and engages employees in the activities of the business.

It is an axiom that "effective people and effective organizations do a few things very well." In an earlier segment, we discussed the myth of the well-rounded person; so it is with companies. In general, if the business model is relatively simple, widely understood and skillfully practiced, people and thus the organization will perform better.

So what is it like to be an employee in such a company? First and foremost, Joe or Joan employee knows who the CEO or president is and what he stands for. In most companies, regardless of their size, Joan or Joe has been in a meeting where the leader articulated the core beliefs of the culture and they know at an emotional level that he practices these beliefs and does not blow big clouds of blue smoke when speaking to employees. "Frank" and "honest" are two words I hear to describe such a leader. It is also likely that there is a mechanism for Joan or Joe to communicate concerns about such things as product quality or customer service up through the chain of command without the message being garbled or lost.

When Joan or Joe comes to work every day, they have an expectation that they will be treated with respect, but also that the bar for performance will be set high. They know that their immediate manager will be a good communicator and coach and give them plenty of timely, accurate feedback about their performance. They know that laggards and whiners, who they dislike, will not be allowed to spread their misery to their co-workers. They will understand the nature of the business and how their job contributes to the quality of the product or service.

Jack Welch, author of the business book, *Winning,* and former CEO of GE, has published a follow-up book discussing the most frequently asked questions in meetings where he discussed the earlier book. About 60 percent are related to career development. So Joan or Joe can expect that the company and her/his manager will invest in the technical and interpersonal development of the employees skill set.

I have a colleague and client who is CEO of a company with about $100 million in sales. He notes, and I agree, that most companies are really operating at something around 40 percent of their innovative and productive capability because of the generally poor way their employees are managed. The basic business principles of leadership and management are well understood, but practicing these ideas is hard work. It's easier and more fun to just manage "by the numbers." To those of you who do this, be advised that more leaders in companies are beginning to understand and use their "human capital" more wisely.

Go To:
Organizations and Management (2.1)
Leadership Is an Important Organizational
Performance Driver (3.1)
Practicing Executive Wisdom (3.18)

Understanding the Job as a Social Contract

The job is an important element in most of our lives. Much of what we think, do and feel carries home from work into our private lives, and thus our job has a significant impact on the quality of our lives. Anyone who has had either a great or a miserable job can attest to this observation.

In general, the job contributes to our lives in three major ways. First, it provides us with an identity. Often when people ask us who we are, we reply by saying what we do. One of the most difficult adjustments for people who have lost their jobs is trying to answer that question. Second, the job provides us with a social environment filled with co-workers. Many of these people will become friends as well as colleagues and constitute an important part of our social-support system. Because of the entry of women into the workplace in the past decades, most neighborhoods are largely empty during the day. This has resulted in the workplace essentially becoming a neighborhood. Third, the job provides us with an income. Those of you who have worked with me know that I am fond of quoting Mae West: "I've been rich and I've been poor, rich is better."

The most striking characteristic of this social contract is how rapidly it is changing in the modern workplace.

Given the importance of jobs in our lives, it is interesting that many people do not really understand jobs in the social context of work and the organization. A job represents a powerful, interdependent relationship — a quid pro quo — between two parties, employer and employee. It is clear that many people involved in both aspects of this social contract have lost sight of the importance of these interdependent responsibilities. Understanding the nature of this relationship and how it is changing can help us understand some of the fundamental economic changes that we read about every day. Therefore, let us examine this social contract in some detail.

There seem to be four basic elements to the halves of the social contract that we refer to as a job:

Employer provides:
- Compensation
- Working environment
- Tools
- Fair management

Employee provides:
- Time
- Skill, knowledge, experience
- Best effort
- Participation, involvement

At the most basic level, the employer promises to provide a fair package of direct and indirect (fringe) compensation; a safe, clean, well-lighted working environment; the tools (technology) necessary to do a good job and competent, fair management. The employee promises to provide the agreed-upon number of hours of attendance, his/her skills, knowledge and experience, the best possible performance and a commitment to be actively involved in continuously improving the quality of products and services.

The most striking characteristic of this social contract is how rapidly it is changing in the modern workplace. Every aspect of this relationship is changing, most in reciprocal ways. Let's examine some of these in some detail.

Many knowledgeable observers would agree that the expansion of fringe benefits is over and that the contraction has begun. The most powerful outside forces driving this change are global competition and the accelerating cost of health care. Simultaneously, many companies are beginning to introduce incentive systems that create a direct relationship between quality and quantity of work and compensation. The intent of such programs is to give employees more ownership and involvement in the business.

Much is happening in the structure of work-time. Such innovations as flextime, four-day weeks, eight-, 10- or 12-hour work shifts and job sharing are being introduced. In addition, many organizations are studying how to retain the talent of senior workers by providing something more than the old practice of retiring people. The intent of these changes is to improve productivity by building work hours that better meet the needs of employees in the varied family structures and developmental eras of people and of our society.

Go To:
Driving Quality Improvements with the
Internal Customer Model (1.17)
What's Your Proper Fit in the Workplace? (4.3)
Surviving and Thriving in Changing Environments (5.3)

4.8

Skills Needed for the Job Can Change Employment Landscape

A national issue that is receiving much attention is concern about the skill, knowledge and experience of the American workforce. Many observers report that some workers are not educationally prepared to fill the high-technology, information-dense jobs of the future. More companies are investing in their people through a variety of internal and external educational practices. In fact, corporate spending on education rivals the combined annual budgets of our public schools.

One of the primary driving forces in the world economy is the ever more rapid introduction of technology into the workplace. Some of us are old enough to remember work settings without computers; now they are an integral part of most work settings. The introduction of technology can quickly alter an organization's competitive advantage; it can also create very stressful working conditions by accelerating the pace of work. The transition from mail to fax to e-mail to texting dramatically illustrates this change.

Along with the concern about education in a technology-driven economy, many people are writing about what they perceive to be an erosion of work values, the so-called entitlement attitude of some workers. Businessmen and women note that workers are not as motivated as in past decades and unfavorable comparisons are often made to other work cultures, particularly on the Pacific Rim. Many believe that a substantial portion of workers is not giving its best effort. Coupled with this perception is the belief that many corporate executives have broken the social contract by increasing their compensation to unreasonably high levels.

Perhaps the most profound change we are undergoing is in the last two elements of the social contract: positive management and personal responsibility. Not many years ago, the idea that part of the social contract was an expectation of fair management would have been considered absurd in many circles. People were thought to be drones, interchangeable parts to be tightly fitted into job descriptions that explicitly defined their role. The responsibility of managers was to direct in a top-down fashion. A quality-driven competitive economic environment has thoroughly discredited this philosophy of management. Today, an essential ingredient of the effective organization is the ability to manage rapid change. The positive management of change is usually referred to as continuous quality improvement and demands the active involvement of all the parties involved in a business endeavor: managers, employees, vendors and customers.

It is time to make clear that the coin titled 'rights' has an obverse side titled 'responsibilities.'

Why then are so many managers and employees in the workplace reacting poorly to these dramatic and often positive changes in the social contract? Perhaps it is because many on both sides of the contract do not understand the central role of personal responsibility in this change.

The United States has just come through an important stage in its historical development. It was a period that might be best described as the Age of Equity and is often characterized as the quest for social justice. It is not unfair to say that these enormous gains in equity have come at some costs. The major cost is that in our need to apprise people of their rights we have neglected to educate them to their responsibilities. We see many examples of this in our society: The propensity to sue rather than negotiate, the skepticism and cynicism many people exhibit toward our institutions, a greater willingness to attack and confront than to listen and problem solve and a tendency for single issues to mindlessly drive decision making. In short, an increasing trend away from reason, moderation and cooperation.

Thus, for at least the past three decades our society has focused its attention on the rights of the individual, often it seems, to the detriment of society at large. It is time to make clear that the coin titled "rights" has an obverse side titled "responsibilities," and that these two fundamentals must be held in balance. Your rights end where my nose begins and vice versa; therefore, to accomplish anything, we must focus on working together. This mutual interdependence of responsibilities is what is often referred to as a social contract, and the job is one of the most important social contracts in our society.

The emerging national imperative to improve the quality of services and products by altering the roles and responsibilities of managers and employees is a fundamental change in every aspect of the social contract known as employment. It is a refocusing of the personal and professional responsibilities for every person in the workplace. Because this effort promises to produce gains in competitiveness as well as improve the quality of work life, it is imperative that we inform and involve people at every level within the organization in this effort.

Go To:
Driving Quality Improvements with the Internal
Customer Model (1.17)
Organizations and Management (2.1)
Surviving and Thriving in Changing Environments (5.3)

Aid Understanding by Defining the Job as a Social Role

In the two previous segments, we spent some time examining the job as a social contract, essentially a deal between employer and employee. The nature of this quid pro quo has an important effect on the productivity of an organization. Looking even more in depth, we can also examine the job as a social role.

I once heard a mental-health professional note that one definition of mental health is having a robust repertory of social roles and knowing when to use them appropriately.

A social role is a set of integrated knowledge and skills that are appropriate to a particular situation. Most adults have a number of social roles. Some of these are broadly defined, such as spouse, friend or parent. Others are more closely defined, such as minister, manager or employee. Still others, such as police officer, physician or attorney, are defined and protected by law, license and regulation. Enacting these roles without the formal permission of government is often illegal. For example, practicing medicine without a license is a crime in first-world countries.

When we consider jobs as social roles, it produces some interesting insights. The explicit definition of roles is essential to the development of an effective workplace. Such definition not only has the effect of improving individual and group productivity, but also reduces the level of unnecessary conflict within the organization. There is compelling evidence that much internal conflict in organizations derives from inappropriate expectations resulting from misunderstandings of colleagues' roles and responsibilities. Thus, a critical issue in the development of effective working groups is the shared redefinition and mutual understanding of roles and responsibilities. Clarifying roles is a relatively easy exercise that is often conceptually difficult because it requires us to define the essential elements of our jobs.

There is a trend in the management literature to define roles in terms of their responsibilities rather than as a set of tasks. This is a reaction to the over-definition of roles as explicit tasks, particularly in job descriptions. When an employee whines, "I don't do that, it's not in my job description," we often assume this to be an example of an "entitlement mentality." But management may have inadvertently contributed to this problem by making the job description too explicit. The knee-jerk correction for this often results in the absurdity of "and other duties as defined." This inappropriate unbalancing of rights over responsibilities is not good for productivity.

There is a trend in management to define roles in terms of their responsibilities rather than as a set of tasks.

By refocusing away from what workplace lawyers define as their "rights," (only the things in the job description) to responsibilities, we alter the unspoken contract from my rights to our responsibilities. Remember, your "rights" end where my nose begins, but our responsibilities are highly interdependent.

A favored technique in new management practice is to define the core responsibilities of jobs. These elements of the job, if not accomplished, cause it to collapse. For example, one of the core responsibilities in my job (which is also my company) is marketing and sales. No sales, no work, no job and no business.

Developing a method to invite employees to explicitly define their core responsibilities results in their prioritizing the elements of their job, having a tool to communicate mutual expectations with their colleagues and beginning to rethink the amount of time spent in each key portion of the job.

Perhaps the most critical time for this re-definition to be carried out is when we promote someone into his or her first managerial position. I often suggest that companies conceptually treat such a promotion as a career change because the responsibilities, expectations and skills required are radically different. An article in the *Harvard Business Review* by Linda Hill titled "Becoming the Boss," illustrates the performance problems resulting from an unrealistic set of expectations about the role of manager.

If you believe as I do that most people in the workplace want to do a good job, then helping them to understand the job is an important step in the journey to a high performance organization.

Go To:
What's Your Proper Fit in the Workplace? (4.3)
What Are the Characteristics of a Great Workplace? (4.6)
Improving Your Personal and Professional Productivity (5.1)

So, You Just Lost Your Job! Now What?

The other morning I reached for a glass and it slipped out of my hand and shattered on the floor. It fell as if in slow motion, but there was nothing I could do about it. Both literally and metaphorically this is what happens when you lose your job. It happens unexpectedly, there's nothing you can do about it when it happens; your shock is followed by anger, regret and resignation. Then you're left to pick up the pieces.

A couple of decades ago, it was much more unusual to encounter people who had been "separated," and many people were ashamed to share that they had been "let go." These days, this is not the case. We live in a turbulent economy that is continuously creating and destroying jobs, and many people have had the "interesting" experience of involuntarily losing their jobs. I once heard a speaker state that the probability of being fired during a contemporary work-life is now about 50 percent. So what do you do when you come to work on Friday morning and don't have a job on Friday afternoon (which is how it usually happens)?

The first and most immediate issue is to manage the emotional shock. Losing a job is an enormously negative emotional experience, and most people report that it is so painful that their brain basically shuts down and they don't hear much after the fatal words, however kindly they are spoken. Remember, it is very important, throughout the fog of your being escorted

The probability of being fired during a contemporary work-life is now about 50 percent.

out of the building, to behave as graciously as you possibly can in these circumstances. This is not the time to throw a tantrum or do something that you will regret later. If you manage to retain some presence of mind, you might try asking if you can be allowed to come in later to remove your personal items when your former colleagues are not present. This is much less painful. Or, if you see this termination coming, you might have some negotiating ploys in mind. Many times, companies would rather do a negotiated resignation than a termination (especially if it's for cause).

When you leave the building, do what you must to regain your wits. You may cry, scream (with the car windows up) or pound the steering wheel. Then, your first decision is: Who are you going to share this with (not where is the nearest bar, although that's an option)? Now is the time for a good friend or an understanding spouse, or if you are really lucky, an outplacement counselor who will know how to help you deal with the hurt or whatever mixed emotions you are experiencing. You need to talk about this with a person you can trust. Not talking, bottling it up inside, is a very poor tactic and a poor predictor of how well you will handle being unemployed and getting your next job. Whatever you do, your family needs to know, including children if you have any. This event will have an immediate impact on their lives, so you must get them in this new game.

You need to recognize that you are going to go through a grieving process and this is natural. You'll likely experience denial, anger, defeat and soul searching. It's very important to get through this process and not get stuck in one stage (don't stay angry forever). The length of time to go through the process differs for each person. The next two segments will outline some tactics for moving on to your next job.

Go To:
One-on-One Feedback is Vital for Your Employees (1.2)
Coaching to Improve Performance (1.6)
What's Your Proper Fit in the Workplace? (4.3)

How to Find a Job After Being Fired

Losing your job has a significant impact on your life. You lose your income, you often lose your friends and, in most cases, you lose a large chunk of your identity.

Recognizing these things as they happen, and watching out for pitfalls that result, can not only help you to weather the loss, but can put you on the road toward finding a new job in a more effective, efficient manner.

First, no more paycheck and the loss of your employee benefits (from free coffee to health-care coverage) is a big hit. It's time to do some rigorous financial planning, and a good tactic here is to hope for the best and prepare for the worst. When the economy is in good shape, the median time to find the next job is about 15 or 16 weeks and it can be much longer. This means there is a 50 percent probability you will still be unemployed in 4 months. Time to give some serious thought, discussion and planning about how to pay the bills. With good fortune, you may have some severance and you may qualify for unemployment compensation.

Second, your work friends are going to be very reluctant to speak with you. Some people say that when you are fired you find out who your true friends really are. There is some truth to this, but in fairness to most of your former colleagues, they are feeling very badly because they have a job and you don't, and they really don't know how to start a conversation with you. You must reach out to them. The best way to do this is to be very open and honest, and not angry, about your new status. Bad mouthing your former employer serves little purpose and it can decrease your chances for the next job. Deal with the emotion, let it go and move on with your life. These relationships are very important; they can be instrumental in helping you find your next job. You will need a support system, so why not use the one that existed in your former company.

Third and most importantly, you have just lost your identity. The most negative aspect of this event for many people is that it calls into question who they are. This is a major hit to your self-confidence. It is essential for you to quickly re-frame your thinking about yourself in such a manner that you now have a new and temporary career: selling yourself to a new employer. This re-framing about who you are is easier for some than others, but is essential because it drives how we talk to ourselves about ourselves. Our self-talk has a huge influence on how we think and feel about ourselves and how we perform. If you can make the mental move to your new job, which is getting your next job, it will have a big effect on your mental and emotional state in the next few months.

Some people say that when you get fired you find out who your true friends really are.

This is the time to perform two tasks: establish a big-picture perspective and take stock of your priorities. Most of us tend to focus on negatives first, and the loss of a job is a big negative. Take time to think of the positive things in your life, and you may also want to remember other losses you have experienced. Compared to many, a job loss will seem minor. While you are thinking about positives, think about your strengths, what you know you do well.

Also, take stock of what matters the most to you in a job and in your life. Is it the town or city you want to live in, or the industry that you want to work in? Maybe it is the balance among work, family and personal time that you crave. By doing this, you're picking up the pieces and moving on.

Go To:
What Is Your Attitude Toward Work? (4.2)
Surviving and Thriving in Changing Environments (5.3)
Self-Talk to Success or Failure? (5.4)

Finding a New Job Is a Group Effort

Searching for a job is not a solo endeavor, it is an ensemble effort. Here are some tips to get you organized and to get others involved. The key to success is to take control of this situation by doing things, by acting. It helps if you have a plan to guide your actions. Consider the following:

Write down the names of three to five people who know your business skills and that you trust. Have a long lunch with each and explain your situation. Get their input. Their comments and suggestions will surprise you. If you know someone else who has lost a job and found a new job, contact that person. Understanding their experience can help you manage yours. Make a list of people you know that you can contact. Establish your network. Focus on the area where you want to work and live. Follow wherever your network takes you.

Communicate continuously and fully with your spouse and family. They are your primary support system. This is a "we" project, not an "I" project. They can help you a lot and you'll enjoy the time you spend with them.

Don't try to work eight hours a day on your job search. This will make you crazy and you will spend too much time spinning your wheels. Build a schedule for your week. Allocate time to do things you love but don't get much chance to do because you were at work. For example, spend more time with your children and spouse, walk, swim, play tennis, especially during your low time of the day. For many people, reading is very therapeutic. Be disciplined. Schedule your time and stick to the schedule. Set goals (three or four a day — not too many) and reward yourself when you accomplish them. Think about working on your job search four days a week. Take Friday or Monday off or alternate days each week. Consider looking into temporary work, paid or unpaid.

Always focus on your positives, your strengths and not your weaknesses. Write them down, post them and refer to them when you need reinforcement. If you are still unemployed six to nine months after the fateful day, be prepared for a stress reaction. It may manifest itself in many different ways. To estimate how, ask yourself how your parents react to stress. Have your partner or best friend watch for changes and let you know.

All human behavior is about three things: thoughts, feelings and

MOTIVATION AND MORALE, JOBS AND JOB LOSS   171

Searching for a job is not a solo endeavor, it is an ensemble.

actions. Monitor your thoughts. How are you talking to yourself? If it's in a negative way, use some mental tools to stop the negatives and start the positives. Keep in touch with your emotions. You are now at high risk for reactive depression. If you get too far down emotionally, talk to your doctor about a brief course of anti-depressants, or see a counselor; talking about this does help make it better. Don't try to be the heroic Lone Ranger; you don't have a silver bullet. Feeling lousy makes it pretty hard to perform, and the new drugs are effective with few side effects. Take action, do things and keep moving. If you slow down or stop, you may get stuck and have big problems. Remember, you can have significant influence on your thoughts, feelings and actions.

Maintain the network of people you have lunch with to share your triumphs and setbacks. Good friends are best in bad times. Make sure you keep in touch with these people, particularly when you are low, because you will have ups and downs and you need their support most when you are down.

If you want an independent assessment of your strengths, or just need positive reinforcement, check into *StrengthsFinder 2.0* by Tom Rath. It will give you a good self-esteem boost.

Remember, this experience will make an interesting cocktail party story to tell in the future. Make sure you keep it in that context now. Also, many people, on being interviewed about the "separation" years later, report that it was one of the best things that ever happened to them. It forced them to carry out a serious review of their lives and make changes that resulted in marked improvements in the quality of those lives. Only your actions in the middle of this crisis can ensure such an outcome.

Go To:
A Multi-Dimensional View of Motivation and Morale (4.1)
If You See a Bathroom, Use It! (5.2)
Self-Talk to Success or Failure? (5.4)

Unit 5:
Personal Development

Without exception, people who perform well in the workplace and in their lives are those who are continuously working to become better at what they do. Mediocrity results from inattention to one's life and work How often have we heard the phrase, "Jane has 25 years of experience. Unfortunately, she has one year of experience 25 times?" The pace of change in the modern world means that everyone who doesn't want to be Jane must be a lifelong learner or else they will rapidly become obsolete. These segments present a more personal and psychological perspective of the context and some concrete skills for becoming more effective. If you want an effective bible to guide you through the process of personal development, consider Stephen Covey's *The 7 Habits of Highly Effective People*.

The first six of these segments are ones that I frequently use in my consulting practice. They provide people with a perspective to focus on what they need to work on to become more effective in their lives. Closely related to these are the first six articles in Unit 4 on Motivation and Morale.
1. Improving Your Personal and Professional Productivity
2. If You See a Bathroom, Use It!
3. Surviving and Thriving in Changing Environments
4. Self-Talk to Success or Failure?
5. Coping with Difficult Situations
6. Take the Time to Stop and Reflect on Success

The second set is focused on the incipient entrepreneur and on the challenges of conceiving of, starting and growing a business.
7. Key Ingredients Make up Successful Entrepreneurs
8. So, You Want to Start Your Own Business — How to Decide
9. How to Succeed as a Startup
10. Growing a Business Is Different from Starting a Business

The penultimate segment reviews the issues of being a member of a partnership and the final segment re-examines the idea of retirement.
11. Making Business Partnerships Work
12. What, Me Retire? Why Should I Do That?

Improving Your Personal and Professional Productivity

The term "professional" is one that is used to describe many different qualities of people at work.

For some, it refers to years of education and degrees acquired. For others it is defined by salary, and yet for others it refers to the apparent importance of a person's title. The definition that I subscribe to defines a professional not based on these elements, but on performance in the workplace and community. From this perspective, professionals are people who function in three characteristic ways.

The first characteristic of a professional is integrity. The simple definition of integrity is doing what you say you are going to do when you say you are going to do it. Unfortunately, some people we work with often will say one thing and then do something different. Think about the people you work with whom you respect and trust. They are almost certainly people who carefully monitor what I call their "say/do ratio." What they promise, they deliver, and if they cannot you are soon informed. For such people "the check is in the mail" is not a joke.

This say/do characteristic is likely the most important foundation of self-esteem.

We are all sensitive to our co-workers' say/do ratios in the workplace and most of us prefer to work with people who have high say/do ratios, people we can trust.

The second characteristic of effective functioning is a personal commitment to quality. It is not so important what you do so long as you do it the very best you can. The road to mediocrity is filled with people who just cut a little corner, and then another and another. These are people who, through their own behavior, have made themselves second-rate.

This commitment to doing your best also means a long-term commitment to your own continuing education. In a time of rapid changes in almost every aspect of the workplace, we must strive to improve our competency by investing in our greatest resource, ourselves. As a person who does many seminars, I find it interesting that participants often comment that the people who need the training most are not in attendance.

The definition of a professional is based on her performance in the workplace and community.

The third characteristic of effective functioning is sensitivity, people skill or as it is now labeled, emotional intelligence. We live in a world of people. To the question, "What is more important, who you know or what you know?" the answer is — yes. Both are important. The world would be a very empty place without the people who surround us. Many people seem to lose sight of this fact. We can influence the world around us, and our own world, through our behavior. A cheerful greeting, a smile, a bit of sincere praise or a word of thanks will create a more pleasant world for us to work in.

Consider the segment in Unit 1: "To Improve Productivity, Try Saying Thank You." Remember, what you give is what you get. I see far too many people in the workplace who seem to operate on the philosophy of "when in doubt, scream and shout." Such people create the angry worlds they inhabit. Treat me with respect and I will reciprocate. Such behavior has a positive side effect. It puts us more in control of our lives. We are acting, not reacting, and this reduces stress.

The triad of integrity, quality and sensitivity is a behavioral definition of a professional. Every day in the world of work, I see such people. Their behavior defines them as people to respect, to trust and as people who can get things done through others.

Go To:
To Improve Productivity, Try Saying Thank You (1.7)
The articles on ethics in Unit 2 (2.10-12)

If You See a Bathroom, Use It!

It's a remarkable thing to have a grown-up child, especially if you have reached an adult-to-adult relationship. My daughter and I were having a conversation recently about life lessons learned in school. She mentioned a particularly fine teacher who transmitted two important principles. The first was, "Life is not always fair," which is self-explanatory. The second was very insightful: "Do what I mean, not what I say." This is an important principle that acknowledges the fact that much of our language is misspoken, so if you recognize this and adjust your behavior, you will be a better communicator and colleague. The principle also sends the message that literal interpretation of the spoken word will be viewed as either passive aggressive or smart-ass.

I was surprised and delighted to learn that she also remembered some lessons from her father. One was, "If you see a bathroom, use it." This of course is not just about foreign travel, or later life, but is rather a metaphor about perception and action. Discussing and reflecting on this quip, it occurred to me that most of the successful people I have known and worked with have these two propensities in abundance.

"Seeing the bathroom" is optimism or what some might call the "silver lining phenomenon." There is research showing that people who have realistic optimism tend to have higher-quality lives than those with a pessimistic outlook. This distinction holds up across a rather wide range of outcomes. However, our concern in this segment is with managers.

The Chinese have a wonderfully telegraphic pair of ideograms (if you read Chinese) that eloquently capture this idea. The symbols mean "time is propitious" and a Chinese-English dictionary states, "This is the critical point of crisis and opportunity which connotes the conditions under which change is likely to occur, and the conditions whereby some opportune moments distinguish themselves from the countless undistinguished moments of history."

When I started my business in 1984, it was my intention to use these ideograms as a business logo. At the time, we had a Chinese neighbor who was a university professor and so I showed him the symbols. He was bemused and noted that the meaning of the symbols was "hurry up, go fast." He quickly showed me the correct ideograms and offered to paint them. That evening he came over to our home, mixed the ink and then proceeded to use a lovely long brush to scribe the symbols. Watching him carry out this ritual was an experience that my wife and I will long remember. He then offered the dictionary definition that appears above. This is certainly more elegant than "if you see a bathroom..."

It seems to me that there is more here than realistic optimism. There is the use of connotation rather than denotation, the important distinction between the subtle and subjective rather than the literal. Seeing the opportunity requires the use of complex tacit information that may not be resident in our easy awareness.

The ability to perceive a moment of opportunity is a powerful cognitive skill.

"Opportune moments" tell us that timing is important, that there may be a right moment when an idea, concept or action will succeed, and that the ability to comprehend that moment is a powerful cognitive skill. Effective managers understand the importance of context and how a conversation can have dramatically different effects depending on when, where and how it is enacted.

"Use it!" refers to another key characteristic of effective people. I often challenge clients to consider the hypothesis that in any situation doing something is better than doing nothing. This usually leads to a spirited round of conversation and reflection. Although this bias for action may not be appropriate in every situation, it is a quality that has immediate and long-term effects if you are a manager. First, it puts you in control of the situation. One of my dearest colleagues often notes that if you come to a meeting with a plan and no one else does, you own the meeting.

I once worked with an executive who was leading a difficult public-sector turn-around. His take on this was he could call meetings, make people come and talk with each other and use his planning abilities to begin to rehabilitate the organization — and it worked. Archimedes said, "If I have a lever long enough I can move the Earth." Effective meetings were this executive's lever.

The second effect of "use it" is that when you take action it changes the situation and opens up new options. As a consultant, I have been in many situations where the client and I didn't know the right thing to do, but we did something and this altered the situation just enough to begin the change process. Sometimes organizational change has a trial-and-error characteristic to it, but a controlled trial and error characteristic.

Go To:
Action-Oriented Style (2.6)
What Is Your Attitude Toward Work? (4.2)
Key Ingredients Make up Successful Entrepreneurs (5.7)

5.3

Surviving and Thriving in Changing Environments

Evidence suggests that people entering the workforce today have a 50 percent chance of involuntarily losing their jobs and may make as many as seven or more job changes in their work lives. Also, the rapidly declining half-lives of occupations mean that it is possible to become obsolete very quickly in any knowledge-based business.

Understanding and adapting to this very turbulent work environment requires new skills for people to survive and thrive. Recently, I worked intensively with a company that was actively developing strategies to better confront and manage the change process. They developed a metaphor useful in understanding and communicating change. The metaphor: Change is like a powerful road-paver, the machine with the 12-foot, 10-ton wheels, that is rolling toward you. As you stand in its path, you have several choices, each of which produces different consequences. Examining these choices helps us understand the change process and our relationship to it.

The first choice is to ignore the change and pretend that it does not exist. The result of this strategy is to essentially become road kill, a clear casualty of the change process.

The second choice is to jump off the road and out of the path of the change. This choice means leaving your current workplace or leaving the workforce entirely (e.g. "early retirement"). If you can afford to leave the workplace permanently, this may be an option, however, for most of us it is not. Jumping to another workplace with the hope there will be little or no change is probably not a good strategy. First, it is impossible to predict how stable an organization is from the outside, and second, an organization that is not changing is probably short lived these days.

The third choice is to recognize the oncoming change as a threat and mobilize your energy to resist the change. This probably means that you will be "rapid road kill." Changing systems are often extremely punitive to those who actively attempt to block the change process.

Understanding and adapting to our turbulent work environment requires new skills for people to survive and thrive.

All three of the previous choices are unproductive because each has failed to carefully assess the nature and speed of the oncoming change.

The first general principle for managing the change process is: Proactively learn as much as you possibly can about the whys and wherefores of the oncoming change. Get a clear picture of the change. Why is it headed this way? How fast is it coming? How big is it? Who is steering? Only by being well informed can you understand and adapt to the change. If you are in an executive or management position, the principle additionally means that you should do all you can to keep your people informed, including letting them know what is not known. This is an application of the general principle of open communication: The better-informed people are, the better they function. Becoming informed about the oncoming change gives us the knowledge base to develop personal and organizational strategies to manage the change process.

The second general principle of managing change is: Assertively participate in the change process. Even if you are at the bottom or near the end of a change process, you can make the choice to participate, if only in a small way. This is very important because it actively engages you in exerting some control over your circumstances. Taking collaborative action instantly identifies you as someone who is not denying that change is happening or resisting change, and skilled "change masters" are looking for people to assist in the process. It also gives you some modest control over your life and may permit you to influence the direction and effect of the change in a positive fashion.

Returning to our metaphor, the strategy is to thoughtfully observe the oncoming change and develop a method to leap up into the driver's seat and help steer. Those who are steering the process will welcome your assistance. However, jumping up onto the steering compartment of this paver may be difficult and dangerous. An important lesson for those who are already up there steering: Reach out to others and invite them into the change process.

Many people are studying the oncoming change but see no clear way to leap up into the driver's seat. Those who are steering the change must actively invite more and more people into the process. Carrying this out skillfully is the most difficult aspect of managing the change process and is probably the reason why so much change is simply driven from the top with little participation and involvement from those who are affected. This produces the stress, resistance and other negative effects that are so often the result of organizational change.

Most of managing change is to adopt a proactive mind-set and to become informed and involved. People who adopt such a personal and professional view are more likely to survive and thrive.

Go To:
Beware: Change Imposed Is Change Opposed (1.9)
Engagement and Decision Making (2.5)
Skills Needed for the Job Can Change Employment Landscape (4.8)

5.4

Self-Talk to Success or Failure?

Talking to yourself and answering is called thinking. Talking to yourself and believing that God is talking back is called schizophrenia. The joke has a kernel of truth because self-talk is an important feature of success and failure in work and life.

Most of the productive people I work with have intuitively learned how to use self-talk to improve their performance. Likewise, some people I have coached have enormous difficulty overcoming their habit of negative self-talk.

When I work with people of both persuasions, I am reminded of Samuel Goldwyn's oft-quoted aphorism: "The harder I work the luckier I get." This is an excellent practical example of the process of "framing." Framing is a cognitive skill that defines how we use our minds to define some event in our lives as being positive or negative.

This ability to realistically frame an event in our lives is not hard-wired; it is learned. However, many people have not learned how to use their greatest ally, their mind, to improve their performance. And because talking to themselves negatively has become a well-practiced habit, it is very difficult for them to change. Naturally, I have been searching for a tool to help people make this transition to more realistic and positive self-talk.

Some years ago, a cardiologist named Redford Williams wrote a book with the intriguing title of *The Trusting Heart*. The focus of his book is on the anger and hostility that has been shown to have a deleterious effect on peoples' cardiovascular systems and seems to lead to heart attacks. However, part of the book introduces a set of 12 mental strategies to improve one's self-talk and thus manage behavior. When I first read these techniques I had a "eureka" moment. The lights came on; here was a set of mental tools that I could learn, as could clients, to improve everyday performance.

What I usually do is discuss these ideas with clients and then suggest they read a short article that introduces and reviews these tools. I suggest that they study the 12 and choose two or three that fit their cognitive style.

Here are the ideas: 1. Monitor you cynical thoughts, 2. Confession is good for the soul, 3. Stop those thoughts! 4. Reason with yourself, 5. Put yourself in the other person's shoes, 6. Laugh at yourself, 7. Learn to relax,

> ## In addition to being more effective, people who 'talk to themselves' experience less stress and tend to be physically healthier than others who do not.

8. Practice trust, 9. Learn to listen, 10. Learn to be assertive, 11. Pretend today is your last, 12. Practice forgiving.

In a short segment, we don't have space to discuss all 12, but here are three favorites.

Learning to set your default impression about people to trust them, rather than not trust them, can make living much easier. Generally, my experience is that most people are trustworthy and it's really not possible to initially identify those who are not. Experience with them will answer this question. I have worked with people who initially mistrust people and it takes them a lot of mental and emotional energy to live this way day-to-day. It is much easier to trust people and proceed from that assumption in working with them. Sometimes this will not work, but not very often. If it doesn't work often, you need to find some new friends or colleagues.

Learning to listen has always been a big challenge for me. My mind works fast and I have a distressing and hard-to-control tendency to finish people's sentences. Women in particular don't care for this behavior because it looks testosterone driven, and it probably was when I was young and acquired the habit. I find myself having to make mini-apologies for interruptions that are personally embarrassing.

Practicing forgiveness is a mental habit that can have a markedly positive effect on you. Essentially, this means eliminating the tendency to find someone to blame for everything that happens that isn't just the way you want it. Becoming a consultant forced me to stop this mental jujitsu because in the workplace, blaming people not only demoralizes them, it is a poor excuse for not identifying the root cause of a problem and addressing it. When you don't blame, it gets you off to a better start with most people; you can almost see their relief. Apparently, lots of consultants play the blame card. I often have clients say that they were surprised that I did it with them, not to them.

Effective people have learned to use their minds to control their emotions and actions. Interestingly enough, these same people experience less stress and tend to be physically healthier than others who do not "talk to themselves."

Go To:
If You See a Bathroom, Use It! (5.2)
Surviving and Thriving in Changing Environments (5.3)
Take the Time to Stop and Reflect on Success (5.6)

5.5

Coping with Difficult Situations

From time to time, we all have situations at work where there is a considerable amount of conflict and stress. Often, we either overreact or do not react. In either case, we leave the situation emotionally upset. Clearly, there must be a better strategy than either suffering in silence or blowing our tops. Both of these, if we are forced to use them too often, lead to professional and personal burnout.

Managing conflict is not a skill that most people have in their repertory of behaviors. We have to gain some control over events and people who are causing us to burn out and burn up. Here are three strategies designed to help you manage difficult people and situations.

The first strategy is "breathing" through the situation, using active listening to get some control. First, take a deep breath and fill your lungs, then let the air out as slowly as you can through your mouth. You can do this without anyone noticing.

Make eye contact with the other person, soften your body language and think about a neutral question you could ask that could defuse the situation. Remember, your first reaction to threatening people and situations is to fight or flee. Either reaction only makes things worse for you. So, try to take control of the event by calming both yourself and the event. This strategy works particularly well with teenage children and will work in

> # The focus of these strategies is to allow you to gain more control over your life, particularly on the job. The key is to have a plan, to do something.

other tough situations as well.

The second strategy is to try negotiating or problem solving. This strategy has five steps. 1. Promptly describe your concern about the situation. Don't ignore it, deal with it as soon as reasonable. 2. Use facts to describe the situation clearly and calmly. Keep your tone neutral and stay away from sarcasm in particular. Sarcasm assures that the other person will react badly. 3. Ask for the other person's views. Try to get them involved so you can understand their perception of the situation. Many people cause conflict unknowingly because they cannot take another's point of view and only see things from their perspective. Try to begin a conversation with the other person. 4. Review the facts and generate alternate solutions to the problem or issue. There are always at least two and usually more solutions to any problem. 5. Agree on an option and what each person will do to resolve the problem. This strategy works particularly well with colleagues you work with on a daily basis. Use it and develop a reputation as someone who can get things done in an efficient and sensitive manner.

Sometimes we are in situations where there is little we can do to minimize the negative effects on us. **In this case I suggest the third strategy: "grin and bear it."** The first thing to do is deal with your emotions. Take some time and calm down. Then try to put the event into the larger perspective of your life. Sure, it looks bad right now, but what about in a week? By then it will probably just be the source of a humorous story. Then, try to understand why the situation exists. Remember, when other people overreact they have the problem, not you. Maybe there is something you can do to help them. After all, they cannot be feeling very good about their inappropriate behavior. Find something you can gain from this experience. Often, some of our worst experiences provide us with our most-valuable lessons about living. In this regard, colleagues and friends can help; talk with them about the event.

The focus of these strategies is to allow you to gain more control over your life, particularly on the job. The key is to have a plan, to do something. The people who are the most stressed are those who are most out of control of their own lives. Slow things down and take control. Make others react to you and take some time to smell the roses.

Go To:
Improving Your Communications Through Active Listening (1.3)
What are the Characteristics of a Great Workplace? (4.6)
Self-Talk to Success or Failure? (5.4)

Take the Time to Stop and Reflect on Success

Recently, a college of business gave me the opportunity to spend the semester with a handful of MBA students in a class titled "Effective Managerial Communications." For various reasons, I decided to give a final exam and began to think about how to do that in a fashion that encouraged the students to dig deep and reflect, not regurgitate a bundle of facts.

I have a good friend who teaches in a college of medicine, and I discussed this challenge with him. He shared a final exam experience he had as a student. He was taking neuro-anatomy, a course devoted to learning the basic structure of the human nervous system, thus lots of memorizing. Those who have taken such a course will remember the mnemonic "On old Olympus towering tops…"

He and his fellow students were sweating the final and reviewing the huge chunks of content. When he showed up for the final, the professor, who he remembers with fondness and respect, passed out the blue books and wrote the final exam question on the blackboard: "Discuss pain." Wow, what a question! He said that for about 20 minutes his mind froze up; this was not the exam he was expecting. The question required the students to review and integrate what they knew about a phenomenon the nervous system mediates. What impressed me was that decades later he recalled the experience lucidly. So, I began the quest for an equivalent question for an MBA course on management and communications.

I thought about this problem for several weeks and came up with nada. So, I recounted the story to the class and asked them to suggest possible questions. After a spirited discussion it was decided that they would e-mail suggestions to me. At the next class I shared these and after some discussion decided the question would be: "Discuss success." They had about two weeks to formulate a three-page paper.

Success is not a material thing; it is much deeper and it is felt, not thought; it is unique to each person, and should not be defined by others.

The thoughtfulness of the papers was impressive. I will try to summarize the major themes.

Many began by discussing what the definition of success might entail. Several thought success was best evaluated near the conclusion of a lifetime by reviewing how a person's books balance. Were things better or worse because of their lives? This, of course, took many dimensions. One notable point was "to get what you want but be sure that you don't want the wrong things." Every person noted that success could not be measured by the acquisition of material things but rather by measures of self-satisfaction and happiness. I was reminded of Maslow's pyramid of needs, as much of the discussion was about the concept of self-actualization.

Several made the point that success is not a material thing; it is much deeper and it is felt, not thought; that it is unique to each person, and should not be defined by others. It was interesting that several people mentioned crucibles that had caused them to pause and reflect on the purposefulness of their lives. The birth of a child, an illness and a career reversal were some of the events mentioned.

Another theme was living the best you can and making the most of each day, always guided by one's values. The value mentioned in this connection is being able to do good when possible. I was reminded of a friend who had recently lost his second parent and on reflection noticed throughout his life he had benefited from many "small kindnesses" that people had shown him without any expectation of payback. He realized that it was often many years later before he understood the positive impact these had on his life. Now, he is wondering if he is providing such small kindnesses for others.

For some, success was best measured by respectful relationships with others, both those very close and those in a wider context. Several who were or hoped to become managers noted that the ability to help others develop to their potential was a source of relationship satisfaction. In general, all entered into the spirit of the assignment and the papers mirrored the individual styles of the writers.

Executives and managers often comment that because of the pace of work, there is little time for reflection. These papers highlight the importance of stopping, taking some time to review and reflect and assuring we are on the life path that brings us "success."

One definition that seems to capture the essence of all the ideas was: "To be successful — you must love."

Go To:
A Multi-Dimensional View of Motivation and Morale (4.1)
Improving Your Personal and Professional Productivity (5.1)
If You See a Bathroom, Use It! (5.2)

Key Ingredients Make up Successful Entrepreneurs

Encouraging entrepreneurs to start and grow businesses is a major goal for MBA programs, economic development agencies, venture capitalists and the list continues. In this segment, we will review advice about key characteristics to successfully launch an entrepreneurial business.

Media companies in many parts of the country identify and celebrate the success of local entrepreneurs with a fastest-growing companies event. Such events usually identify and profile a specific number of the fastest-growing companies in their area, highlighting their growth rates and the number of jobs they have created. At one such meeting, the keynote speaker shared the core characteristics of successful startups.

He began by noting that fast companies are about growth, and thoughtfully qualified this by saying the issue was not just growth, but wise growth. Then, with five elements, he defined his meaning of wise growth.

First, to start a successful business you must identify the right moment. How often have we heard it said that timing is essential to success? He drilled more deeply and noted that this really means identifying the right market. Is there a need for this product or service and what opportunities derive from serving this need? In describing the need for his product, a trans-fat-free vegetable oil, he noted how critical vegetable oils are to our lives and how the absence of trans-fats in such products is shown to have demonstrated health benefits. Consider this in juxtaposition to baby boomers who want to live long and be healthy the whole trip. What a moment this is for a company that knows how to build such a product.

The right moment then takes the company to the right product. Knowing the facts about the market, understanding the core competencies of the people and what type of product will meet these needs, makes it possible for the company to develop a product with the quality and at the cost that will make it attractive to potential customers. Assuring there is a good fit between the people and the product is an essential element of running a business.

The third element is illustrated by a terrific Midwestern story. Money is needed to start a company and 25 Iowa farmers saw the opportunity and became venture capitalists. He noted that most startups fail because they run out of money. So, he shared that spending money wisely was the third key element of successful entrepreneurialism. Entrepreneurs are obsessed with cash flow; it is the pulse of their organizations.

Rapidly growing companies are not just about growth, but about wise growth.

The fourth element is great people. Entrepreneurs have a great recruiting advantage because they are able to offer a unique opportunity. Each person in a startup can have an enormous influence on the process of creating something brand new. Not many people have such an opportunity and a powerful self-selection exists that brings motivated, committed people into this game. Those who join but cannot manage the risks and work involved are soon discarded. Natural selection operates rapidly in entrepreneurial companies.

The last ingredient is passion. He stated this was the best job that he had ever had. Imagine what it is like to work in a place where everyone shares this belief and is doing whatever they can to support each other and the larger endeavor. Many people will pass through their lives without having this immensely satisfying experience.

Reflecting on this speech, I was again reminded of Peter Drucker, who said that "the result of a successful business is a satisfied customer." Entrepreneurs create satisfied customers because doing so is about surviving and thriving.

Go To:
Leadership Is an Important Organizational Performance Driver (3.1)
In Praise of Peter Drucker (3.6)
Executive Wisdom: Context (3.14)

So, You Want to Start Your Own Business — How to Decide

One of the remarkable aspects of the American economy is how easy it is to start a business. Often, people who want to venture into the world of self-employment and start their own businesses call me for advice. I usually begin by sharing that I have the best job in the world — for me — and if they successfully start their own business, they can create the best job in the world — for them.

For the right type of person, running your own business is an enormously satisfying experience. You can maximize your strengths and minimize your weaknesses. You can create new, worthwhile and satisfying jobs for people (nearly half of all new job creation in the United States happens in companies with fewer than 50 employees). You can step completely out of the constraints of working for someone (no one can ever fire you). You can make an important contribution to your community. You can create wealth for yourself and your employees. Given all these possible positive outcomes, what are you waiting for?

Starting a business is making the ultimate career change. You begin by identifying something you love, do very well and can develop into a business model you can sell. Only by developing a business you love can you obtain the above-noted rewards. The quest to carry out this change can be great fun. Begin by asking yourself, "What do I do as well as or better than anyone and get personal satisfaction from doing?" Contrary to contemporary myth, successfully starting a business is not a disjunctive change. In fact, people who succeed use skills, talents and motivations that they already possess and then learn how to leverage these attributes. Sometimes, business development may appear a radical break with one's past, and it probably will be organizationally, but those who are successful draw upon their strengths to build their core business.

If you are not yet sure what that business will be, begin your search by identifying two or three people who are insightful, know your work very well and are reflective. Invite them to meet one-on-one and ask an ambiguous question such as: I am at a choice point in my life and I don't know what I want to do when I grow up. Then listen attentively; you may be surprised at what you hear. When I did this many years ago, the first person I talked with advised me to start my own consulting business. My immediate reaction was that the idea was absurd; two years later, I started Langhorne Associates and have not looked back since. Sometimes, trusted others know you better than you know yourself.

If you know what the core expertise is that will drive your business,

---

Starting a business is the ultimate career change.

---

then begin by identifying a handful of people who successfully operate similar businesses. As before, individually share your ideas with them and ask them to tell you the key early elements that made their businesses successful. Put aside your biases and listen; these are successful people and much can be learned from their experiences. For example, one such person advised me to always do my very best work, no matter who the client or what the fee. Later, I learned the wisdom of this advice because good news, as well as bad news, moves very rapidly. Another piece of advice I heard over and over was that it takes about three years to sufficiently cash-flow a business, so be prepared to work very hard those first three years and don't give up too soon. Yet another advised me that business is about sales and if you cannot learn how to sell, you're toast.

Before you launch, find a good accountant, one who can be a trusted business advisor, and then heed her advice. Such a person has seen many businesses succeed and fail. She can give timely advice that will help you become a better businessperson. As before, listen without bias and act on the information. Also, join the local chamber of commerce, get involved and avail yourself of its networking opportunities to increase your visibility in the community. Your accountant can also help you decide on the legal structure to choose for your endeavor. The simplest form is the sole-proprietorship, which is simply adding a Schedule C to your 1040. If you decide to incorporate, there are many options. Further discussion of this topic requires a knowledgeable professional in the area.

One interesting aspect of running your own business is that it can be very lonely. You are now the boss and sharing some kinds of information with your employees can be very risky. It is very important to cultivate a support system because you need someone you can confide in, ask for advice and provide encouragement when nothing seems to be working. When I started, one of my major support persons was a woman who had just re-entered the workforce and was becoming a broker. We discovered there were many similarities in the marketing and sales of our new occupations and would meet frequently and discuss these. We also had a deal to always call the other for lunch when we were discouraged. Remember, the first couple of years can be an emotional roller coaster.

Be prepared to deal with the emotional effects that result from losing many of the aspects of employment that come with a traditional job, such as vacation time, sick leave, health-care insurance and watercooler talk. These no longer exist for you. You are on your own. Everything is your responsibility. For some people this is exhilarating, for others it is terrifying. If you are in the latter group, maybe your future can best be lived working in a more traditional job.

There are lots of studies on the characteristics of entrepreneurs, but the most important characteristic appears to be realistic optimism. Realistic optimism means you believe that you can do it but are aware of and responsive to threats to your success. The business environment provides lots of feedback, and your ability to rapidly adjust your behavior to this feedback is one key to success. Running a business is like good engineering problem solving: plan, do, check and act. You will get some things wrong; learn and fix them. Do these things and your success will propel you on the way to a much more interesting and enjoyable life.

Go To:
Action-Oriented Style (2.6)
If You See a Bathroom, Use It! (5.2)
Surviving and Thriving in Changing Environments (5.3)

How to Succeed as a Startup

Starting a business is one of the most valuable things you can do because you create something of value. You maximize your strengths and minimize your weaknesses. You create new, worthwhile and satisfying jobs for people. You step completely out of the constraints of working for someone. You make an important contribution to your community. You create wealth for yourself and your employees. So now that you have decided to start your own business, how do you succeed?

Perhaps the most important contributors to successfully starting a business are your attitude and willingness to work. Entrepreneurs usually have a strong sense of realistic optimism. They carefully balance risks and opportunities and are committed to rapidly learning from their mistakes and changing their behavior to profit from these lessons. Be very clear; unless you have started a business before, you really don't know how to do it. Your worst possible enemy is your own arrogance. Fortunately, you will be surprised at how many people will offer to help, if you ask them.

One important decision to make when you start is whether to slide or jump. Sliding is staying at your current job and gradually building your business using time off. If you slide, be sensitive to conflict-of-interest issues that may create problems even as you begin. In an ideal slide, you can gradually phase out your traditional employment as the business becomes successful. Sliding is also an opportunity to build a financial cushion for the cash-flow downturns that will occur. Jumping is moving rapidly to full self-employment and has the advantage of making you totally focused on the new business. Many people slide for a bit, and then jump. Another important advantage, but probably not a reason to get married, is having an employed partner who can provide a regular income as well as health-care coverage. It is much less risky for half of a working couple to begin a business.

Early in your business development, you may want to consider hiring a consultant who can advise you how to structure and focus your marketing and sales efforts. Such an advisor may begin by asking what you are selling and to whom. For many entrepreneurs, marketing and sales is often the biggest challenge. On this topic, or any other, if you need help, don't hesitate to find good advice, heed it and act on it. Perhaps the best predictor of business startup success is the ability to rapidly process, learn and re-adjust your behavior when you make mistakes. I once worked with a successful entrepreneur who operated with the philosophy that the mistakes he made were more information-rich than successes and were the quickest way to redesign his business practices to succeed. It is very clear that entrepreneurs are action oriented. They have high say/do ratios — what they promise, they deliver.

The most important contributors to successfully starting a business are your attitude and willingness to work.

One piece of advice you don't usually hear is to be very careful about hiring your friends. Yes, you know them and their skill sets well, but consider that if they don't work out they will be very hard to fire, and at the start if you don't deal with non-performers, they can make you fail. Some friends, unfortunately, will trade on their relationship with you and try to turn the job into a sinecure. Such people are not friends, they are subtle enemies. Remember, if you set initial performance expectations high, this will be a key portion of creating a culture of success.

Perhaps the most fun aspect of a startup is that you have the opportunity to develop the business culture through your decisions and actions. Entrepreneurs often underestimate the importance of maximizing internal communications and don't usually give enough thought to how decision making is going to occur. In the beginning, you will be making all the decisions, but as your confidence in your staff grows, you need to learn how to wisely share decision-making authority. If you insist on making all the decisions all the time, this will eventually become a barrier to growth and will drive away the very best people.

You will be surprised by how attractive working in a startup is for some people. Many people see it as a once-in-a-lifetime opportunity to be a part of something important at the beginning and have a big hand in helping to grow it. These are the people you need to hire.

The success rate of new businesses, those in business five years on, has been improving over the past years, probably because the business environment is more welcoming and there are more support services than in the past. However, one of the most striking features of people who are successful is they are willing to work as hard as it takes. Such people always report that working for oneself is much more satisfying than working for someone else.

Go To:
Leadership Is an Important Organizational Performance Driver (3.1)
If You See a Bathroom, Use It! (5.2)
Self-Talk to Success or Failure? (5.4)

5.10

Growing a Business Is Different from Starting a Business

Every year, more than 600,000 new businesses incorporate, and the number who survive is increasing as more support for entrepreneurs develops. Yet only a small number are able to grow beyond about $10 million, and very few have development trajectories that take them to $100 million. Some of this results from wanting to stay small and remain easy to manage, but too many businesses seem to grow rapidly and appear to suddenly self-destruct.

A study by the Small Businesses Administration showed that cash flow is the single most important measure of success and that the major barriers to growth were poor sales and an inability to handle business growth. There is a size where becoming larger becomes a difficult barrier, and most businesses fail to recognize that growing requires different skills than starting a business.

Starting a business requires constant attention to developing steady, positive cash flow and the importance of sales is obvious to entrepreneurs. What most entrepreneurs fail to realize is that growing a business means learning how to scale, how to grow the business wisely. This

> ## What most entrepreneurs fail to realize is that growing a business means learning how to scale, how to grow the business wisely. This means leadership must focus on the organization as well as the accountant and the customer.

means leadership must focus on the organization as well as the accountant and the customer.

Almost without exception, entrepreneurs succeed because they are extraordinary micro-managers, and this competence is the major reason that growth becomes a success-threatening issue. Building a business means building a management and organizational structure and it means learning to delegate important work to others. Entrepreneurs have little difficulty delegating to accountants, especially if they are not accountants themselves, but they often try to retain control of every aspect of the core business. Beyond a certain size, this is impossible. The issue here is that when you begin, you know everything about your business, and that is reassuring. Eventually, the focus must shift from knowing every detail to understanding the organization is the tool to accomplish the core business.

Here are some warning signs of this growth transition. People, especially the CEO, are not having fun anymore. Key people are not performing as well as they did when you started. Customers and employees are unhappy and the grapevine is turning negative. Internal communication and cooperation are declining. Turnover is still too high. The organization is forming cliques or silos. Employees report that the place is losing its "family feel."

If any of the above is the case, then it's time to begin the transition from entrepreneur to CEO. These events are bad news and bad news doesn't age well, particularly in small companies. The failure to understand, recognize and manage the transition from a small business to a fully functioning corporation can be life threatening to a company.

Leadership is the most important driving force in effective organizations. Knowing this tells us that managing this transition must begin at the top of the organization. If you are the CEO, you cannot make all the decisions all the time. You need to be thoughtful in how you deploy your time and maintain your focus on the core elements that are driving the performance of the company.

Typically, you are surrounded by a group of people who started with you and to who you have great loyalty. Now you have to consider if they are the very best people to be in place when key decisions are made and executed. The hazard here is the people who started with you may not become great managers; the needs of the organization may have outgrown them. I often see entrepreneurial companies where several key people have clearly been over-promoted.

Rebuilding a company at the same time you are rapidly growing is a challenge similar to rebuilding a jet airplane while it is in flight. Begin by assembling a small group of trusted advisors, internal and external, and take a hard look at the organization and the people in key positions. Start by examining the warning signs and pose such questions as, did the organization just expand in response to the demands of growth or do you have the best structure in place to grow? Are the people in key positions able to grow with the company? What is your bench strength — do you have people in the pipeline to move into key positions, or have you been hiring to meet immediate needs? These questions will get you started and lead to in-depth conversations.

These conversations can help begin to assess the fundamental strengths of the organization, begin a conversation to identify and address areas that need attention, take the first step toward building a high-performance management group and develop a stronger recruiting and developing program. They also set a pattern of periodically taking a hard look at the overall performance of the company, identifying issues before they become major problems.

Go To:
Beware: Change Imposed Is Change Opposed (1.9)
Managing: What Are Your Expectations? (2.2)
If You See a Bathroom, Use It! (5.2)

5.11

Making Business Partnerships Work

The business partnership is a powerful organizational model and many great businesses are organized as partnerships. The reason is that two or more people with similar interests and complementary knowledge and skills come together and decide to leverage their mutual strengths to create a successful business. The best partnerships occur when these people develop shared practices to jointly maximize their attributes. In the case of couples, often these people are also romantically intertwined and/or married.

Typically, what happens in a business partnership is the people divide the responsibilities in a manner that maximizes their personal and professional strengths. For example, one person may take charge of marketing and sales, whereas the other takes responsibility for operations and administration. We often see responsibility allocation inside and outside the company (i.e. sales and operations). Usually, these arrangements are worked out when the business begins and refined during its early years.

Partnerships, like marriages, can be enormously effective when the allocation of responsibilities is thoughtfully designed and executed. As in marriages, partnerships require constant attention to maximizing direct, frank communication and a clear strategy for decision making (as in yours, mine and ours). However, as the business becomes more successful, each partner is drawn more deeply into his or her area of responsibility, sometimes at the expense of these shared functions. This is most likely to occur as the organization begins to add significant numbers of employees or changes its business model without seriously rethinking how this will affect what have been comfortable and effective working relationships.

By the time the pair or group notices, the relationship may be frayed and in need of significant rebuilding. Symptoms of this might be increased conflict between the principals and among others within the organization, employees playing one partner off the other, the formation of cliques based on reporting relationships and employees reporting unclear or mixed messages from leadership. If these issues persist long enough, they will affect morale and productivity and customers will begin to notice.

In some recent work with a partnership running a very successful small business, changes in the partners' personal lives had spilled over into the workplace and were beginning to cause staff and customer-service prob-

As in marriages, partnerships require constant attention to maximizing direct, frank communication and a clear strategy for decision making (as in yours, mine and ours).

lems. Specifically, they were having difficulty managing a troubled employee. Time spent with them clarifying roles and responsibilities, as well as agreeing to explicit mutual expectations, helped them to reconstruct a collaborative decision-making style. Decisions began to be made and enacted in a more direct and timely fashion, and staff almost immediately noted the improvement. Had the initial situation continued, it might have had serious long-term negative effects on the business.

Partnerships often work well because they can efficiently distribute authority and responsibility to maximize individual strengths. However, they require constant attention, particularly with regard to decision making to avoid conflicts and to benefit from the potential of such a mix.

Go To:
Driving Quality Improvements with the Internal Customer Model (1.17)
Engagement and Decision Making (2.5)
Understanding the Job as a Social Contract (4.7)
Skills Needed for the Job Can Change Employment Landscape (4.8)

What, Me Retire? Why Should I Do That?

Retirement is an artifact of the 20th century. Before the 20th century, people worked until they died, at very early ages compared to today, and if they were mentally or physically incapacitated, they were cared for by their extended family.

When I was a college student working summers in a lead smelter in western Montana, I saw remnants of this practice. Older workers, usually in their late 50s or early 60s, were put into jobs, such as cleaning the bathhouse, that didn't require much muscle or mental effort before they retired. In those days, people in their late 50s were a lot older than such people are today.

One of the fruits of the old industrial economy was that it created jobs that allowed people with little training but a willingness to physically work hard the opportunity to earn an income that propelled them into the middle class. Collective bargaining was a powerful mechanism for social change and supported this trend by essentially re-balancing the power relationship between labor and management. However, as we have moved through the industrial economy to the service economy to the information economy, this type of physically hard-work, high-wage job is disappearing. Some blame this on globalization, but it is technology that is doing it. Jobs are becoming more and more mental, requiring less and less muscle. Immigration fills the need for low-wage, hard-work jobs as never before. Welcome to the future.

Community colleges are full of young people who have learned this lesson the hard way. They didn't pay much attention in high school, graduated sometimes and then went to work — at or too near the minimum wage. Soon, they noticed that others making a better wage and getting promoted had more schooling. Community colleges have provided these people with an opportunity to bootstrap themselves. The contribution of the community colleges is a higher-education success story of the past couple decades.

This movement of jobs from muscle to mental is changing the nature of retirement. Today, most people are not old when they are 65 and they have a good chance of living into their 90s. This was unheard of three generations ago. People in the early 20th century retired, had a few years and then died. These days, people who have gone to school for many years have the opportunity or the risk, depending on their situation, of being retired longer than they were in the workforce. Comparisons of contemporary workers and their ancestors who served during the American Civil War show that people today are physically and cognitively healthier than several generations ago.

The movement of jobs from muscle to mental is changing the nature of retirement.

Consider the traditional pattern of retirement in the 20th century. One day you are fully employed and the next you are not and have a gold watch or some other trinket to show for 30-plus years of work. From our perspective in the early 21st century, this looks really unnatural. So, what are people doing? Many are not retiring. For some, retirement is boredom. Their work is mental, they have valuable experience, have developed the habit of work and they tend to be very good employees, if somewhat more expensive.

Many companies that are in a hurry to shed their older workers are discovering that younger workers are much more likely to quickly depart to another company and have a different work ethic that some managers find incomprehensible.

Some potential retirees are remaining in their jobs but are phasing down to three or four days a week. Others are joining a company job pool of "sort-of-retirees" and temping for their companies at their former compensation and sometimes at nearly full-time. As the baby boomers retire, more companies are offering the above opportunities, but only to their better employees. I think we can expect these trends to accelerate.

Some are retiring and restarting. They are leaving their employers of many years and starting their own businesses, sometimes in competition with their old employers. Those who succeed find a niche that maximizes their strengths and allows them flexibility to manage their time.

Some are retiring, doing the travel and golf thing, getting bored and coming back into the workforce. The hazard of this reentry pattern is that they can never come back at the level they left. They can, however, leverage their experience to make a qualitatively different contribution. One example is a school superintendent who re-enters and becomes the director of a high performance private pre-school.

Consider also the relatively affluent retiree who, rather than re-entering a traditional job, begins a new career, or perhaps starts a small non-profit to address a social or economic issue within the community. This is an attractive option for successful business people.

What is essentially happening here is that the baby boomers are adding a new phase to what can be thought of as the longitudinal career pattern. These phases are: school, apprenticeship, journeyman, preparation for retirement and retirement. This new career element is somewhere between full-time employment and full-time retirement. Given the health, youthful outlook and affluence of this cohort it will be interesting to see what new career options they create in the near future.

Go To:
If You See a Bathroom, Use It! (5.2)
Surviving and Thriving in Changing Environments (5.3)
Take the Time to Stop and Reflect on Success (5.6)

Topics Index

These are groups of segments related to the listed topic. They are ordered sequentially from the simplest to the most complex.

Problem-Solving Index

These are the most-frequent problems front-line managers encounter in their day-to-day work based on surveys of clients. These segments can be used to prepare you and then you can use them one at a time to introduce ideas to employees and/or managers, following up with conversations and coaching. You must be well prepared for these one-on-one interactions. Remember, people don't change quickly, so be tenacious about asking for improvement. If no change occurs, then you will probably be moving to progressive counseling and so begin to build documentation. I recommend you build your basic skill set by reading and understanding:

One-on-One Feedback is Vital for Your Employees (1.2)
Candor is a Valuable Trait in Successful Leaders (1.5)
Improving Your Communications through Active Listening (1.3)
Managing Troubled and Troublesome Employees (1.13)
Respectful Behavior (2.4)

If you are working one-on-one, I suggest you become familiar with the first six segments in Unit 5: Personal Development. Thoughtfully choosing one of these can really make a difference if the timing is right.

• The most frequently cited issue is giving **timely, accurate feedback** or professionally giving constructive criticism.

One-on-One Feedback Is Vital for Your Employees (1.2)
Candor Is a Valuable Trait in Successful Leaders (1.5)
Improving Your Communications through Active Listening (1.3)
To Improve Productivity, Try Saying Thank You (1.7)

Build your skills with the first three segments, then use the "thank you" segment with the person if appropriate and follow-up with another one-on-one.

• Managing **people with poor attitudes** and others with the entitlement mentality (what has the company done for me lately) is another common problem.

What Is Your Attitude Toward Work? (4.2)
Understanding the Job as a Social Contract (4.7)

Begin with a feedback session and ask the person to read the attitude segment. Discuss it at the next meeting. Based on the reaction to these two segments, follow up with selections on motivation (4.1-6) or on the basic nature of the job (4.8-9).

• **Poorly performing** direct reports or peers are often the most difficult issues for many managers. Difficult people can bring down morale and productivity. Not being able to manage poor performers can be a career stopper.

Managing Troubled and Troublesome Employees (1.13)
Action-Oriented Style (2.6)
Principles vs. Rules (2.7)
Coping with Difficult Situations (5.5)

Before you embark on progressive counseling, make sure you know your policies cold and that your manager is supporting you.

• Helping **people work together** so they can be productive is another challenge.

A Multi-Dimensional View of Motivation and Morale (4.1)
Surviving and Thriving in Changing Environments (5.3)
To Improve Productivity, Try Saying Thank You (1.7)

Begin with these three, then go to the relevant sections and select material as appropriate. You will probably be using group process here, so review "Managing Better Meetings" (1.8). Be sure to stay focused on the main issue.

• Managers have many questions about motivation, such as how to come up with more creative ways to **recognize performance,** how to find time to improve individual and team performance, and how to increase employee engagement. Consider starting any initiative along these lines by reading the first six articles in Unit 4: Motivation and Morale, Jobs and Job Loss. Understanding motivation can then take you to practices and ideas you can use and share with employees. If you want to know how to do something with employees, it's usually a good idea to ask them selectively. The first nine segments in Unit 2 can be of help here. Pay particular attention to:

Managing: What are Your Expectations? (2.2)
The Power of Information (2.3)
Respectful Behavior (2.4)
Engagement and Decision Making (2.5)

• Developing a workplace where people are more focused on their personal **professional development** is an important issue. These three segments will give you the context to begin to address this issue.

Improving Your Personal and Professional Productivity (5.1)
Organizations and Management (2.1)
It Is Important to Give Employees Vital Information (3.10)

Development Index

These are sets of developmental series designed to improve the knowledge and skill levels of various groups within companies. Experience indicates the best way to use this material is to begin with one article at a time, preferably in sequence, and then have a key manager — the person's immediate manager is preferable — follow up with a one-on-one or a small-group meeting. In either format, begin with a round robin question such as, "What was your most important take-away from this segment?" The key idea here is to start a conversation about the topic of interest. Before you start such a process, you may want to review segment 1.3, "Improving Your Communications through Active Listening" and segment 1.8, "Managing Better Meetings." As you become more familiar with the material in the text, you may want to consider designing a series to meet your unique needs.

When you are comfortable with the 75 segments, you can design unique series for individuals or groups within your organization.

New hires: New hires, especially those just out of school, often bring misconceptions about the nature of work.
Improving Your Personal and Professional Productivity (5.1)
What Is Your Attitude Toward Work? (4.2)
Understanding the Job as a Social Contract (4.7)
Skills Needed for the Job Can Change Employment Landscape (4.8)
How are Your Relationships in the Workplace? (4.4)

New managers: This is a lengthy series and is the foundation for an internal development program for new managers.
Introduction to the Management Practices unit.
The Basics of an Effective Management Style (1.1)
One-on-One Feedback Is Vital for Your Employees (1.2)
Improving Your Communications through Active Listening (1.3)
KISSing and Chunking: A Magical Method for Better Communications (1.4)
Candor Is a Valuable Trait in Successful Leaders (1.5)
Coaching to Improve Performance (1.6)
To Improve Productivity, Try Saying Thank You (1.7)
Managing Better Meetings (1.8)
Beware: Change Imposed Is Change Opposed (1.9)
Managing Troubled and Troublesome Employees (1.13)
What Predicts Managerial Success (2.13)

Personal performance: Use these on yourself or with a direct report or colleague that you are coaching.

Improving Your Personal and Professional Productivity (5.1)

If You See a Bathroom, Use It! (5.2)

Surviving and Thriving in Changing Environments (5.3)

What Is Your Attitude Toward Work? (4.2)

Respectful Behavior (2.4)

Self-Talk to Success or Failure? (5.4)

Coping with Difficult Situations (5.5)

Take the Time to Stop and Reflect on Success (5.6)

Manager into leader: Use these with a high-performance manager to help him understand and develop his leadership potential.

Transitioning from Manager to Leader (introduction)

Introduction to Management (book introduction)

Leadership Is an Important Organizational Performance Driver (3.1)

A Multi-Dimensional View of Motivation and Morale (4.1)

Organizations and Management (2.1)

Principle-Centered Leadership Has Benefits (3.2)

A Personal Model of Leadership (3.3)

Leadership as an Organizational Process (3.4)

Leadership: A Journey of Self-Awareness (3.5)

What Are the Characteristics of a Great Workplace? (4.6)

Principles for experienced managers: More-experienced managers could benefit from discussion of these principles.

Organizations and Management (2.1)

What Are the Characteristics of a Great Workplace? (4.6)

Managing: What Are Your Expectations? (2.2)

The Power of Information (2.3)

Respectful Behavior (2.4)

Engagement and Decision Making (2.5)

Action-Oriented Style (2.6)

Principles vs. Rules (2.7)

Tactical to Strategic (2.8)

Courage: Managers into Leaders (2.9)

Change management: Understanding how to develop participation in the workplace is an important development stage for high-performance managers.

Beware: Change Imposed is Change Opposed (1.9)

Engagement and Decision Making (2.5)

Managing Better Meetings (1.8)

Driving Quality Improvements with the Internal Customer Model (1.17)

Developing individual employees: This material is particularly helpful to a manager who is developing the key one-on-one skills that help her build a great operating unit.

One-on-One Feedback is Vital for Your Employees (1.2)

Improving Your Communications Through Active Listening (1.3)

Candor is a Valuable Trait in Successful Leaders (1.5)

Coaching to Improve Performance (1.6)

Motivation: This series is useful for anyone who is interested in understanding the complexity of motivation.

A Multi-Dimensional View of Motivation and Morale (4.1)

What is Your Attitude Toward Work? (4.2)

What's Your Proper Fit in the Workplace? (4.3)

How are Your Relationships in the Workplace? (4.4)

What are Your Motivators and Demotivators? (4.5)

What are the Characteristics of a Great Workplace? (4.6)

Respectful Behavior (2.4)

To Improve Productivity, Try Saying Thank You (1.7)

HBR Index

Executive development: A set of fundamental readings

Over the years, I have had the opportunity to work with many fine managers and executives. These are smart, thoughtful people who think and reflect deeply about what it is they are doing in their organizations. I have often shared information with them that helped both of us think and talk about the whys and hows of managing and leading. Recently, with the stimulus of leadership development, I have begun to systemize these readings into what I consider a set of core articles that provides a base of knowledge about managing and leading. Thoughtful study and conversation about this material can provide the basis for formulating a personal philosophy and practice of management and leadership. All of the following articles can be found in the *Harvard Business Review*. (http://hbr.harvardbusiness.org).

CONTEXT:

The Coming of the New Organization. Peter Drucker. January-February 1988.
Don't be put off by the date; in this prescient article, Drucker describes today's workplace and introduces the idea of the knowledge worker.

Management and the World's Work. Peter Drucker. September-October 1988.
Drucker places management into its current context and ends with the most lucid definition of what management is that has ever been formulated. This classic "must read" is an article I return to often for guidance.

MANAGEMENT:

Managing Oneself. Peter Drucker. March-April 1999.
History's great achievers — a Napoleon, a daVinci, a Mozart — have always managed themselves. But they are rare exceptions, so unusual in both their talents and their accomplishments as to be considered outside the boundaries of ordinary experience. Now, most of us, even those with modest endowments, will have to learn to manage ourselves.

Becoming the Boss. Linda A. Hill. January 2007.
The earliest test of leadership comes with that first assignment to manage others. Most new managers initially fail this test because of a set of common misconceptions about what it means to be in charge.

Pygmalion in Management. J. Sterling Livingston. September-October 1988.

A manager's expectations are the key to a subordinate's performance and development. This article explains why some managers get such great performance from their people whereas others get so little.

Managing Your Boss. John J. Gabarro and John P. Kotter. January 2005.

If you forge ties with your boss based on mutual respect and understanding, both of you will be more effective. The idea that you have responsibility for managing the relationship with your boss is one that effective people understand intuitively.

Who's Got the Monkey? William Oncken Jr. and Donald L. Wass. November-December 1999.

The burdens of subordinates always seem to end up on the manager's back. Here's how to get rid of them. This is the classic and definitive article on delegation.

One More Time: How Do You Motivate Employees? Frederick Herzberg. January 2003.

In this HBR classic, Herzberg helps us to understand the complexity of human motivation. The data in this article are aging, but the basic principles, especially the discussion of hygiene and motivation factors, are timeless.

What Great Managers Do. Marcus Buckingham. March 2005.

This is an approach to managing that derives from the positive psychology model and focuses on maximizing peoples' strengths. It's a pretty good model for new managers.

LEADERSHIP:

Level 5 Leadership: The Triumph of Humility and Fierce Resolve. Jim Collins. January 2001.

What catapults a company from merely good to truly great? A five-year research project searched for the answer to that question, and its discoveries ought to change the way we think about leadership. The most powerful transformative executives possess a paradoxical mixture of personal humility and professional will. They are timid and ferocious. Shy and fearless. They are rare — and unstoppable.

What's Your Story? Herminia Iberra and Kent Lineback. January 2005.

All of us construct narratives about ourselves — where we've come from, where we're going. The kinds of stories we tell make an enormous difference in how well we cope with change.

Crucibles of Leadership. Warren Bennis and Robert J. Thomas. September 2002.
Everyone is tested by life, but only a few extract strength and wisdom from their most trying experiences. They're the ones we call leaders.

Primal Leadership: The Hidden Driver of Great Performance. Daniel Goleman, Richard Boyzatis and Annie McKee. December 2001.
We've known for years that emotional intelligence improves results — often by an order of magnitude. Now, new research shows that a leader's mood plays a key role in that dynamic — a discovery that should redefine what leaders do first and best.

Discovering Your Authentic Leadership. Bill George, Peter Sims, Andrew N. McLean and Diana Mayer. February 2007.
We all have the capacity to inspire and empower others, but we must first be willing to devote ourselves to our personal growth and development as leaders.

What Makes An Effective Executive? Peter Drucker. June 2004.
Great managers may be charismatic or dull, generous or tightfisted, visionary or numbers oriented. But every effective executive follows eight simple practices.

ORGANIZATIONS

Simplicity-Minded Management: A Practical Guide to Stripping Complexity Out of Your Organization. Ron Ashkenas. December 2007.
I don't see many good articles on organizational design. This is one. Start with the self-assessment.

The Discipline of Teams. Jon R. Kazenbach and Douglas K. Smith. March-April 1993.
The definitive article on high-performance teams. Take particular note of their definition of team vs. group.

Building Your Company's Vision. Jim Collins and Jerry Porras. September-October 1996.
This is the best article I know to solve the confusion about vision, mission and strategy and is based on their best seller *Built to Last*. This is where the term BHAG (big, hairy, audacious goal) originated.

References

Byham, William C., with Jeff Cox. *Zapp! The Lightning of Empowerment*. Fawcett Columbine, 1998.

Collins, Jim, and Porras, Jerry I. *Built to Last*. Harper Business, 1994.

Collins, Jim. *Good to Great*, Harper Business, 2001.

Covey, Stephen. *The 7 Habits of Highly Effective People*. The Free Press, 1989, 2004.

Damasio, Antonio R. *Descartes' Error: Emotion, Reason and the Human Brain*. Grosset/Putnam, 1994.

Drucker, Peter. *The Effective Executive*. Harper, 1967, 2006.

George, Bill. *True North: Discover Your Authentic Leadership*. Jossey-Bass, 2007.

Lynch, Peter. *Beating the Street*. Simon & Schuster, 1993.

Peters, Tom, and Waterman, Robert. *In Search of Excellence*. HarperCollins, 1982, 2004.

Rath, Tom, and Clifton, Donald O. *How Full is Your Bucket?* Gallup Press, 2004

Rath, Tom. *StrengthsFinder 2.0*. Gallup Press, 2007.

Rath, Tom. *Vital Friends: The People You Can't Afford to Live Without*. Gallup Press. 2006.

Schonberger, Richard J. *World Class Manufacturing: The Lessons of Simplicity Applied*. The Free Press, 1986.

Welch, Jack, and Welch, Susy. *Winning*. Harper Business, 2005.

Williams, Redford. *The Trusting Heart: Great News about Type A Behavior*. Times Books, 1989.

To purchase this book go to:

www.BeyondLuck.net

To learn more about John Langhorne go to:

www.langhorneassociates.com

To visit John's blog go to:

http://langhorne.wordpress.com

To learn more about the Corridor Media Group go to:

www.corridorbiznews.com